Making Memories

A celebration of the life of
ANNE PRESSLY

By Randy Dixon, Christina Muñoz
and research assistant Lauren Scott

Published by
Arkansas Times

PRINTED IN THE UNITED STATES OF AMERICA

ISBN 978-0-615-31847-9

10 9 8 7 6 5 4 3 2 1

INTRODUCTION

On October 20, 2008, Arkansans learned of the brutal attack on KATV anchor and reporter Anne Pressly in a report on Channel Seven News:

> *"We have sad news to tell you about this morning. KATV's Anne Pressly is in the hospital after an attack in her Little Rock home. Police tell us Pressly was found at around 4:30 a.m. this morning with severe wounds. Police say there are no suspects but that the attack may have come during a robbery, because her purse was missing. We would ask that you keep Anne in your thoughts and prayers."*

The following days were frenzied as the incident quickly became international news. It was especially trying for her friends and colleagues at the television station who were dealing with a personal tragedy while still covering a major news story.

The outpouring of love and compassion was overwhelming. KATV was flooded with cards, gifts and flowers for Anne. Her desk was literally covered with signs of support. KATV's web site received thousands of emails from around the world.

The story became even more tragic on October 25, 2008, when Anne died as a result of her injuries. Her death, the memorial services, an ongoing police investigation and the subsequent arrest of a suspect all made national news. After time, however, the press corps left Little Rock to move onto other news leaving her friends and her community to deal with this personal loss. Everyone dealt with their grief in different ways.

A part of the mourning process was the difficult decision to clean out her desk. It had remained untouched for several months. We had continually put off the dreaded task, knowing that it would make her passing more of a reality. As we removed items and placed them in boxes, we came across a stack of handwritten post-it notes. Anne had a habit of writing a daily Bible scripture and would stick it to her computer screen. It gave her strength and encouragement. As we read through the notes, we were impressed that she had kept them all these years and thought sharing them might inspire others. The idea for this book came from seeing those hand-scribbled scriptures.

A scholarship foundation has been established in her name to reward outstanding future broadcast journalists. All proceeds from this book will benefit that fund.

—Randy Dixon,
Christina Muñoz

CONTENTS

FOREWORD

The news of Anne Pressly's death hit hard. I had known Anne from her earliest days at KATV-TV in Little Rock, the ABC affiliate that has been the launching ground for many successful news careers of major network "stars." She was an ideal young television reporter in that she was strikingly beautiful, but she was also a very hard-working and intelligent young lady who fearlessly pursued her stories and was a genuinely professional and competent journalist. She was ambitious without being ruthless and was persistent in asking questions without being rude and obnoxious.

The savage and senseless attack on her in her own home would have been a shocking crime regardless of her being a local celebrity, but for those of us who had gotten to know Anne, whether professionally or personally, it was hard not to be angry and vengeful to the kind of hideous thug who could act with such cold cruelty to someone who was so compassionate and kind.

Arkansas is a small state and people tend to have a sense of community. Local TV news personalities and political figures are the most visible people and therefore are greeted by first name by strangers on the street as it seems we know them.

In Anne's case, I did know her. She was often assigned to cover me in my capacity as Governor and followed my campaign for President, even traveling to distant states to tell the local folks how their homegrown candidate was doing. Her contagious smile, engaging personality, and cordial and courteous demeanor were disarming, but in no way meant that she was less than a focused journalist determined to get the story, whatever it was. It would be easy to say I liked her, but more importantly, I respected her and knew that while I couldn't expect her to throw softballs and do "feel-good" stories about me, she would be fair and try to find the REAL story. In a word, she had class.

The attack on her and her subsequent death hit me hard for another reason. My own daughter was the same age. In fact, my daughter had been to a wedding shower just two weeks earlier and had seen Anne. When I heard the news about Anne, I didn't think about Anne the promising television personality, but rather as someone's little girl. Anne was blessed with wonderful parents who deserved better than to to have to go through the agony they suffered.

Anne is gone, but in her brief life she left an indelible mark on her family, friends, and the wonderful small state of Arkansas. We don't say goodbye, but rather "Good night, Anne, we'll see you in the morning."

—*Mike Huckabee*
Former Governor of Arkansas
and radio / TV talk show host

REFLECTIONS ON ANNE FROM HER MOTHER

Early photo of Anne

Anne was sunshine born into this world. She was my beloved daughter. Anne slept through the night from the first night on ... already amazing us. My friends with babies close to the same age could not believe it! She was so sweet and cuddly that I always held her close. I never wanted to put her down. She was a perfect, precious baby. Anne took her first steps on her first birthday, Aug. 28, 1983. She never stopped running after that day.

She loved Sesame Street — Big Bird was the star at her second birthday party (played by her Aunt Pam, of course!). By age five, Anne was in the top of her class at First Baptist Church Kindergarten in Greenville, S.C. Reading books was something she loved at this age and forever. At the end of the year in first grade, Anne won the math award, science award, reading award and citizenship award. Even at this early age, it was apparent she would always be a leader and never a follower. Anne had a very strong spirit. She was determined and pushed herself. She never had to be pushed for anything. Calling out spelling words was never necessary. She was very detailed and competitive with her peers. She loved to write stories. She loved being silly and playing dress-up and being girly. She took tap and ballet lessons. She learned to play tennis.

During her middle school years, Anne had a keen interest in architecture and home design. She collected books and sketched many plans of her own. She could tell anyone about house design and always had ideas and opinions about houses and what she would do to make a particular one better. She had an eye for color as well. Anne was part of a competitive cheerleading team that traveled from an early age.

Her high school class was the Class of 2000. In high school, she was editor of the newspaper and treasurer of her class. She was a writer for The Greenville News, a member of the Homecoming Court and a cheerleader. She enjoyed playing parts in high school musicals. *Bye Bye, Birdie* was one of them. Her passion for being on stage strengthened her desire to pursue her dream of being on television. Anne was involved with her church youth group and Young Life. She went on several mission trips throughout the United States and helped build houses for the poor. She learned how to snow ski and enjoyed white water rafting.

After visiting 26 colleges across the country, Rhodes College in Memphis, Tenn., was her first choice. Anne pledged Chi Omega sorority and later became social chairman. Anne's apartment there was very hip and very pink. She planned and designed it by herself ... fashion and style were her passions. She developed a strong interest in politics, and was a political science major. Anne would come home to Little Rock during college breaks and stop in at KATV and ask if she could help during the holidays and summers. She began doing anything that was needed and loved every minute of it all! During her junior year of college, Anne had a weekly appearance on KATV's *Good Morning Arkansas*. She landed a speaking part on the soap opera *As the World Turns*.

By her senior year in college, she was in charge of the student interns at KATV. Prior to her graduation from Rhodes College in 2004, she landed her first job as a reporter in Jackson, Tenn. Anne commuted the last six weeks during college finals... she was following her dream. The day after graduation from Rhodes, Anne auditioned for a part in the movie *Walk the Line* and was cast as one of Johnny Cash's first girlfriends. An opportunity opened as a producer at KATV and she dropped out of the movie to jump at the chance to be a part of the family she loved at KATV.

Anne bought and restored a condominium and "flipped it" on her own and then purchased her first house. She made her own drapes, painted the walls ... she was never afraid to try anything. The vision and design was all Anne. She rescued many dogs, and had two beloved blonde Cocker Spaniels, Clementine and Daisy. She loved to participate in charity events from fashion shows to the Polar Bear Plunge. She involved many friends to help make rafts out of cardboard to float for charity, to cheer runners at Race for the Cure and to be involved in Paws on the Runway. She loved the opportunity to interview people from President Clinton and Vice President Dick Cheney to Dixie Carter, Naomi Judd, Maya Angelou and Robin Roberts. Anne was asked to audition for a part in the movie *W*, directed by Oliver Stone. She was cast as Ann Coulter, a political strategist.

She always seemed to be cheering or dancing. When Anne entered a room, it was electrified. She was beautiful inside and never recognized her outward beauty. She was full of laughter and could make you roll on the floor. My favorite memories are of her laughing, with tears spilling down her face. There was not another smile like Anne's ... to have been chosen to be her mother was such a privilege. She was my precious daughter and her life touched thousands and will continue to change the lives of others.

She was a great example of a strong young woman who lived the Christian life without pretending to be something else. She was the real thing and a blessing to all of us who knew and loved her. She was a testimony to all of us. For all of us who loved Anne, our lives will never be the same. Our hearts are forever broken. The world is dimmer without her beautiful smile. The phrase "making memories" was taught to her by her great-aunt, Jacqueline, who reminded us all, in everything we do, we are *making memories.*

Anne was truly an amazing young woman. I feel that all of us who knew and loved Anne were truly in the presence of an angel. From a conversation with Beth Moore, who calls us to remember Hebrews 12:1: Anne is among the "great cloud of witnesses" who is cheering us on as we go forth spreading the Gospel ... running our race. Anne has run her race and passed the baton to us. And in the end, we will see her again, on the other side of the cross.

— *Patti Cannady*

Anne's first publicity photo

FIRST IMPRESSIONS

There is no question that if you ever met Anne Pressly, she left a lasting impression on you. One of the most enduring memories of Anne was most likely your first encounter with her. She was larger than life with an over-the-top personality. Anne was certainly anything but subtle. Her loud voice, voluminous hair, and gorgeous smile captured your attention without demanding it. Many times she was heard before she was seen. Although her extreme enthusiasm could sometimes come across as brash, it was always forgiven. Whether you knew her intimately or casually, personally or professionally. she made a memorable impact.

"All I remember about Anne is ENERGY. I was at the station when she came in as an intern and it was GO, GO, GO all the time with her and such a HUGE personality. Sometimes it made it difficult to focus on your job, but it was always entertaining. At social gatherings it was the same way with her. Of course for Anne, even work was a social gathering. When she came back as an employee, you quickly saw the maturity she had gained; but she also was the same high-energy woman she was as an intern. Enthusiastic about everything. That is what I will always remember about Anne."

—*Justin Acri, former KATV sports anchor*

"The first thing that comes to mind about Anne is that she was loud. But in a good way. I remember I was sitting in the newsroom and I heard her before I saw her. I just remember thinking, 'I wonder if she's like that all the time?' And after knowing her for about four years, yes she was. What started out as a little bit of hesitation, and maybe because of that, grew into what made me love her most. She just put herself out there. So I really think that's what drew people to her. It's what intimidated people at first, but in the end it's what made people love her."

—*Amanda Manatt, KATV reporter*

Heather Crawford,
Finley Turner and Todd
Yakoubian with Anne

"My first impression of Anne was 'calm down.' It's like 'slow down, Anne,' because she just burst into the newsroom, 'What up, Peeps!' Gosh, she just, she owned the room when she walked into it."
—*Todd Yakoubian, KATV weekend meteorologist*

"I remember the first time I met her at Channel 7. She was interning for the summer and was sitting in the newsroom. All of the interns were looking eager just to do something to impress somebody. From the very beginning, Anne was always the one who commanded the attention. Whether in a large group or a small setting, your eyes went directly to her. I'm not sure if it was the bright pink Dolce & Gabbana dress or stark white smile she would flash or maybe it was when she stood up and said, 'Hey everybody. I'm Anne. Can I follow you around today?' I remember thinking, she has a great look, a bubbly personality ... if she's smart and can talk well, she'll go far."
—*Jason Harper, former KATV morning host*

"Over the top! When I first met Anne Pressly I remember feeling intimidated by the big smile, big hair, and big voice. I was a new reporter, and she was one of many interns, but I never would have guessed it. I assumed she was an employee because of the way she carried herself and the way others interacted with her. I had just moved to Arkansas from Minnesota and was unfamiliar with the local dialect. I remember not being able to understand everything Anne, or 'Sassy' as she was known then, said. Partly because of the Southern accent, and partly because I had never met anyone like her and was trying to figure her out as she talked. Although her booming 'Hey y'all's' seemed strange and almost bothersome at first, they later became one of the things we all learned to love about our larger-than-life Anne."
—*Christina Muñoz, KATV news anchor*

"When I first met her, I was an intern and she was just the most welcoming person ever. She had just a warm smile and wanted to take you in. She wanted to show you how the ropes work. She was always the one that was like 'you want to go out on a story?' Of course, the first few weeks I was like 'I don't know about this.' I was so nervous about asking anyone to do anything, but she really put me at ease. She was beautiful inside and out."
—*Courtney Dixon, KATV production assistant*

"The first time we met she said 'WHAT!!!' Then I saw the blonde hair and the 32 teeth and I began to get an appreciation for her because she did not fit the dumb blonde stereotype. She was a very good writer and very detailed in her stories."
—*James Dokes, KATV communications supervisor*

"The first time I met Anne I remember thinking wow, she is loud. I had just started here and I was nervous about how people were going to receive me and what they would think of me and she was one of those who welcomed me with open arms. Right off the bat, she was being sarcastic and joking around and you kind of wondered if it was all a performance or if it was really who she was. But she never let up so you quickly figured out, 'Oh my gosh she's like this all the time.'"

— *Dale Nicholson III, KATV weekend sports anchor*

"How can anyone possibly forget the first time they met Anne Pressly? I clearly remember the day. I had just arrived in Arkansas to interview for a reporter position. I remember spending a short time in the morning meeting and then Randy Dixon introduced me to the girls in the newsroom. I heard a loud, Southern accent coming from the back of the newsroom and saw a group of girls huddled together laughing. I was introduced to Kate Sullivan, Michelle Rupp, and Anne Pressly. Back then Anne was an intern but she seemed just as much a part of the group as anyone. I remember thinking how pretty she was, how she had a lot of blonde hair and how much she seemed to LOVE celebrity gossip magazines!"

—*Jessica Morkert, former KATV reporter*

Jessica Morkert and Amanda Kelton with Anne

"We instantly connected. She was so beautiful and vivacious and just always had a smile on her face. She was always entertaining everyone. She just filled the room. The second she walked in, all eyes were on her. I just instantly loved her."

—*Heather Crawford, KATV anchor/reporter*

"My first impression was she's kind of a scattered brain, but after being around her for a while, I realized she was an extremely smart girl. She always liked to have a good time, and I always liked to have a good time. She was a lot of fun."

—*Mike Herman, KATV photojournalist*

Anne and Heather Crawford

"She just sort of ingratiated herself into this newsroom and she wasn't even involved in it at the time. She would just like show up. And we didn't even realize who she was or what she was doing. My first impression is that she was really tall. A lot of people might not realize that TV makes people look a little different in person."

—*Ned Perme, KATV chief meteorologist*

" She definitely had a boisterous personality. Unlike anybody else in the newsroom. You knew if it was Anne's day off or if she was out on a story because she was going to command some attention, there was no question about that. She was just always in a good mood. We said that about Paul Eells a lot but Anne was always in a good mood, too. She always had an interesting story to tell about her day, always involved everybody in her life and was the center of the newsroom."

—*Scott Inman, KATV news anchor*

" The first impression that I got from her was loudness and not in a bad way, just that she owned the room. It didn't matter what she was saying, her voice carried. And whatever she was saying, people wanted to know what she was saying not just because it was loud but because she was Anne. I think some people misjudged her because she was so loud and flamboyant. They might have thought that she was fake, but I just think she was unfiltered. She was the most unfiltered person I had ever met, and she wasn't afraid to not only be loud, but to live her life out loud. I just think that's why people were attracted to her."

—*Beth Hunt, KATV morning anchor*

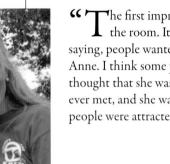

Beth Hunt and Anne

" I remember meeting Anne soon after I moved to Little Rock in early 2007. She quickly struck me as one of the friendliest, happy and beautiful people I had ever met. Anne had an effervescence that was unmatched. She was always excited, always positive and radiated a light that was truly contagious."

—*Samantha Friedman, Arkansas Democrat Gazette reporter*

" Somehow, Anne just kept showing up at Channel 7. First, as a model on *Good Morning Arkansas*. She was a high school student working at Beyond Cotton and showed off clothes. Then she was a guest representing the store. Next, she burst into the newsroom as an intern. She came a couple of weeks early because she was so excited. By the time the other summer interns arrived, she was part of the crew and proclaimed herself as the 'senior intern.' She took it upon herself to conduct the tours of the station for the new students. She returned the following summer for yet another internship. After she graduated from Rhodes, I hired her as my part-time assistant. She did that for a while, but really wanted to be on-air. I advised her to do some time in a smaller market to get the experience to work in Little Rock. She got a job in Jackson, Tenn., as a reporter and was thrilled. However, after working there for a few weeks, she was told she had to sign a two-year, no-outs contract. The contract would also prevent her from working in the Memphis or Little Rock markets for a year after. She was devastated and wanted advice on what to do. I told her not to do it. She was in a bind in that she'd just moved there and didn't have a job if she quit. I happened to have a producer opening for our *Good Morning Arkansas* program. We worked a deal that she could produce during the week and report on the weekends. She was concerned that she had little producing experience and might not do a very good job. She was right. She may have been one of the worst producers in the history of the station. Thank goodness a reporting position opened fairly quickly."

—*Randy Dixon, KATV news director*

" I first met Anne when she interned here. She was so excited to be here at Channel 7 and to be an intern. She was asking a whole lot of questions about what you do, or how do you do this and that. She was always happy. I asked her every day what are you drinking or what are you taking because she was always high on life. You could be having a down day and she could just lift your spirits. She was a lot of fun."

—*Ray Hamilton, KATV photojournalist*

"The first time I met Anne it was on my interview here. Anne really stood out. She came into the afternoon meeting, late, carrying a huge Diet Coke and she was bubbling about something that had happened that day. I remember thinking that girl must be a reporter."

—*Shilo Groover Korzen, KATV producer*

"I first met Anne as an intern at Channel 7. I was nervous and was trying to act professional, and Anne instantly put me at ease and made me feel comfortable, just as she did for everyone. We were on our way to a story, and she loaded me up with sour patch kids (of course), Diet Cokes and celebrity gossip magazines. She told me we needed to catch up on TomKat (Tom Cruise and Katie Holmes)! Anne was a pro at making people feel loved and included."

—*Mallory Hardin, KARK reporter*

"Whew, over the top! Anne's personality ... larger than life. I could remember distinctly when she would come into the newsroom. It would be quiet and all of a sudden you hear 'What's up, Peeps!' Just a bubbly, infectious kind of personality. Crazy girl, lots of good times. Despite having a down day or not feeling well, if you hung around Anne for even a second your spirits would be lifted."

—*Pamela Smith, KATV weekend anchor*

Anne and Pamela Smith

"**A**nne was one of the first people I met when I came to work at KATV. She was an intern and it was my first day as a production assistant. Anne actually gave me a tour of the station. I didn't even know what her real name was because everyone there called her 'Sassy.' I remember thinking, 'Is she really this happy all the time?' Over time, I quickly realized that YES she really was happy all the time. Everyday when she walked through the door Anne had a smile on her face, a Diet Coke in hand, singing whatever song she was just listening to on the radio and would give us all a shout out as she entered the newsroom."

—Jamie Deason, former KATV producer

Jessica Dean and Anne

"**I** was sitting in a word processing class in 8th grade at Pulaski Academy and the door flew open and in walked this very tall blonde. She was two years ahead of me so she would have been in 10th grade. She kind of threw her head back like she always did and she said, 'Hey!' I just remember looking up and going 'who's that?' The whole room stopped to look at her ... and she never lost that. I think that's something that you're born with, and I think she was born with it. I know she had it when she was in 10th grade, and she had it when she was 26 years old. And even someone who was in the 8th grade ... how old are you then? 14 maybe? I even knew that at that very moment when she walked in. She was just always Anne. She knew exactly what she wanted and where she was going, and I think people just followed her lead a lot of the time. That's just who she was, she had that characteristic and that charisma."

—Jessica Dean, KATV reporter

"**H**er enthusiasm was just infectious. I remember the first time I met her, I mean she could make you want to do things you didn't particularly want to do because she was so enthusiastic about it."

— Dale Nicholson, KATV president and general manager

"**I** remember her as an intern. The loud, almost obnoxious intern screaming and yelling. And the first thing I guess I remember is her being called 'Sassy.' "

—Chris Scott, KATV producer

"**A**nne was going out on a story at the Capitol. I was an intern, kind of nervous and kind of scared and she just took me under her wing. She said 'Katrina, you're coming with me.' I didn't even know her and she just acted like we were cool right then. We went to the Capitol and met Tim there and she introduced me as the newest editor. Embarrassed, I asked Anne to please stop saying that and she was like, 'Oh girl, you got it I promise you got it.' Even then, when I was a nervous little intern, she was giving me confidence and she didn't even know me a day."

—Katrina Dupins, KATV producer

"**V**olume. Volume of her hair, volume of her voice. Just larger than life. Louder than life. Fun personality. That's what I remember, fun."

—Jason Pederson, KATV consumer reporter

"When I first met Anne she was an intern. I was working in the River Market and I remember thinking 'who is this loud girl?' She was loud and ready to work. She was real, she was a joy. It was 'who is this firecracker?' When she opened her mouth it was like boom! She had that boom."

—Tyrone McIntosh, KATV studio production

"Anne Pressly. I don't think anyone quite knew what to make of her the first time they met her. Right off the bat it was just big hair, big smile, big laugh ... the girl was truly larger than life."

—Kristin Fisher, former KATV reporter

"I think she was an intern and I remember coming into the newsroom and seeing this person flying around and I'm thinking who is this? The news department has always had a lot of energetic interns but there was something about Anne that really just kind of stood out. All it takes is that one, first impression and you're sold for life."

—Mark Rose, KATV general sales manager

"The first time I saw her, I won't ever forget it. Noel (my husband) and I were looking at this house and were considering buying it. We had driven behind the house that we were looking at and hadn't seen anybody out so we turned around and drove back in the ally. Anne, being the good girl that she was, had walked out and was standing at her mom's mailbox watering her flowers. I remember thinking who is that beautiful girl? I don't think I had seen anyone that pretty. It stuck with me. I think she had workout clothes on and her hair was thrown up in a ponytail. But she was just so pretty."

—Joan Early, KATV reporter

"My first memory of Anne was when she was interning at KATV. I was doing audio at *Good Morning Arkansas* and this 'intern' came bouncing in and laughing with that patented screechy Anne Pressly laugh. I looked at Ken Watson and we both said, 'Oh, no ... it's going to be a long summer!'"

—Billy Cannon, former KATV satellite truck operator/editor

"When I first met Anne she was an intern. I remember that Anne was always laughing. She was always cutting up and laughing."

—Wayne Cox, KATV sales account executive

"I sent Anne an e-mail message the first week that I worked here. Within 2 minutes, I got a reply from her saying how excited she was that I was here and that she would come to my desk to get me and take me on a tour of the building. About 5 minutes later, she showed up at my desk and the first thing I thought was that it seemed like she was just lit from within. She was so bubbly and friendly and just genuinely a good and very happy person. She took me over every inch of KATV and introduced me to every single person we came across as we went through the building. She told me to be sure and let her know if there was anything she could do to help me and that she was just so glad that I had let her know I was here. She couldn't have been more friendly or welcoming."

—Melinda Carelock, KATV sales account executive

"My first memory of Anne was when she was interning at KATV ... this 'intern' came in laughing with that patented screechy Anne Pressly laugh. I looked at Ken Watson and we both said, 'It's going to be a long summer!'"
—Billy Cannon

Anne with Jamie Deason and Amanda Kelton

"**M**y first impression was what a personality. What a big personality."
—*Mark Farrell, KATV executive producer*

"**I** first met Anne while working as a *Nightside* production assistant at Channel 7. She was home from Rhodes for the summer and working at the station. At first, I was completely intimidated by her. She carried the nickname 'Sassy,' and it certainly fit. Someone described her once as 'bigger than life.' That's the only way to describe her. She was constantly laughing and making other people laugh. I envied that quality."
—*Amanda Kelton, former KATV producer*

"**I**'ll never forget the first time I met Anne. I was walking into the newsroom from covering a story in Dumas and it was one of those sweltering Arkansas summer days and I was so glad to be back in the air conditioning ... and turning the corner bounds Anne Pressly. Gorgeous, tall, South Carolina blonde and she immediately threw out her hand and said 'Hi I'm Anne,' with all the friendliness and magnetic energy that we would come to know as uniquely Anne. I could be wrong, but I think she would go on to intern longer than any other intern at KATV. Every summer she came back. Christmas ... she came back ... as soon as she graduated ... she came back. It showed her drive ... how much she really wanted to be in the news business and a part of KATV. She was destined for great things ... not just because she was so beautiful, friendly and smart ... but because she was willing to work as hard or harder than anyone else."
—*Kate Sullivan, former KATV news anchor*

"**S**he had me at 'Hey, y'all!' Over the years our friendship blossomed, but from the start it was definitely my attention she had. From the beginning, her entrance into any room was quite show-stopping. It seemed nearly impossible to work through the early morning 'Hey y'all's' from an intern who'd clearly just consumed two Red Bulls. (I learned the Red Bull trick down the road). Admittedly so, it didn't seem like a friendship that would stand the test of time, but as the old adage suggests 'time will tell' ... and boy did it ever."
—*Tomeca Sloan, former KATV producer*

"**G**orgeous, long legs. Hollywood legs. Going to go far, going to go places. I'm a guy so what would you expect, of course."
—*David Bazzel, 103.7 The Buzz radio host*

"**S**he was wearing this white furry jacket and she had this beautiful blonde hair and this huge smile, and I just thought this girl looks like an angel! I was just taken away. You could not meet Anne without taking a step back and just saying, 'Who is this girl?' She was amazing, and her overall presence was just something you could not miss."
—*Angela Rachels, KATV assignment editor*

*Anne at 17
during a modeling
session*

Making Memories **17**

Anne and Marcus McDonald

COVERING THE NEWS

There was also a serious side to Anne. She was a smart, hard-working and dedicated journalist. She treated every assignment with equal importance, no matter what it was. She covered just about every kind of "hard news" story: politics, natural disasters and trials with serious and thorough reporting. And she showed equal enthusiasm with the lighter features like festivals and sporting events. She immediately excelled in her newest role as anchor and morning show host. Her presence on live television was so captivating because she made it look so easy. For those who worked with her, she made covering the news so much fun.

"All stories were big to Anne. Every story you did meant something to Anne. She always got a little something out of everything she did. Whether it was a trash story or covering the President of the United States. Every story was big to Anne. She never put one above the other. Everything had a joy and a meaning in it for her. And therefore you, too, would get something out of it."

—Marcus McDonald, KATV photojournalist

"I remember one weekend she was subbing for Pam. It was the weekend of the Arkansas Derby when Curlin, the big horse, was racing. Anne was going on and on about how much she loved Curlin and that was her horse. The race was on in the weather center and she was sitting there at her desk. She was oblivious to what was going on talking about how great Curlin was and I said 'Well, he's about to race right here!' She turns around and says, 'There's a race today?!' So then we go down to the set and she said, 'I have been looking forward to this race all day' on the air. She was talking about how excited she was about the Arkansas Derby and that she's had this date circled on her calendar. Then Todd goes, 'You didn't even know there was a race today!' So we busted her out on the air a couple times pretty good."

—Dale Nicholson III, KATV weekend sports anchor

"**M**y favorite memory of Anne, by far, was when I was following Mike Huckabee for the South Carolina primary with her and Brian Ferguson. She gave us the 'Anne Pressly Tour of South Carolina' telling us what to avoid and what to visit if we ever came back. She was one of the hardest working reporters because of her willingness to hit the ground running. She even helped us chase cables when we had video problems, something she did not have to do. She never hesitated to ask what she could do to help. I covered everything from tornadoes and flooding to politics with Anne, and she still, even under high-stress times, managed to laugh that laugh we all grew to love. Watching her with people she was interviewing, she was a true professional. She always understood the emotion of the story."

—Billy Cannon, former KATV satellite truck operator/editor

"**W**hen Dick Cheney came to Arkansas she calls me and says 'Dude, you're not gonna believe what just happened!' She said they were down at Mack's Prairie Wings (in Stuttgart) and that the State Police were there. She walks up to them and they say the Vice President is in there. Well, she waltzes right in there and interviews him! Only Anne could do that. But I'll always remember her calling me and saying 'Dude, you're not going to believe this story!'"

—Mark Farrell, KATV executive producer

"**A**s competitors, Anne and I ran into each other on a lot of stories. We often covered the same stuff. One of my first impressions of her reporting skills came when we covered an eight-week trial together. The first day of the trial, opening statements were long and very detailed. The case contained dozens of charges and three defendants. It was a VERY involved and complex story to tell on TV. Of course I was blown away by Anne's fabulous clothes, gorgeous thick blonde hair and bubbly personality, but I was MOST floored when I saw her rendition of opening statements air that evening. We were both doing live remote reports from outside the courtroom, working without computers and producers at our fingertips. I was amazed at a graphic of an umbrella Anne had the station build for her. She called it in from the field and explained to the graphic artist that she wanted that umbrella built with each spoke to show a different category of criminal charges. That was so smart, so artistic and made it so easy for the viewer to understand. Anne could grasp the complexity of any story and break it down to simple terms for anyone to understand."

—Melissa Dunbar-Gates, KTHV reporter

"**I** watched Anne kind of critically because I knew her mom and knew a lot about her and she was fairly young. I watch everybody kind of critically and she was so good. She was really good regardless of where you put her in the story. She didn't have bad days and you don't have a lot of people in this business who have good days every day. I thought she was just really talented and actually got better a lot quicker than I thought she would."

—Steve Sullivan, KATV sports director

"Anne and I started producing at about the same time. I was doing *Daybreak*, she was doing *Good Morning Arkansas*. To be honest, I thought she was horrible. She couldn't time a show to save her life and what appeared to be her dumb blonde routine drove me crazy. But what I did notice is that she had a way with people. She connected. When Anne moved on to reporting I thought it was great; I didn't have to deal with her on a regular basis … little did I know that we would once again be reunited in the evening newscasts. Not everything was always pleasant between us. I can't tell you how many times she was late with her story, way over, or just blew me off all together. But then what seemed like overnight, something changed. Maybe it was her … but the more I think about it, I think it was me. I had connected. Before she moved back to the morning schedule I thought she had truly hit her stride. Her stories became more compelling and I couldn't wait to find out what she was going to come up with next. She had a way to pull the best out of every story and make it relate to the viewer. For the first time I truly hated seeing her go. I knew once Anne began anchoring on *Daybreak* that it wouldn't be long before she would be moving on. You could tell that she was on a roll and that nobody was going to stop her. She was headed places."

—*Patrick Green, KATV producer*

"Anne had the most amazing way with people. Anyone. She could make people feel at ease. Find a common ground. I could travel the state with her and she would ask, 'Where y'all from?' And she could connect: 'Cabot? Go Panthers!', 'How about those Dewitt Dragons! Lovin' some Lonoke Jackrabbits!' I think she knew the mascot of every high school in the state."

—*Randy Dixon, KATV news director*

"I had been here 30 years and had never been on camera. My birthday was the 29th of February and Anne came up and said, 'We need to do this story on leap year babies.' Kyle's not here and she couldn't find anybody, would I do it? I don't know, I finally gave in and was finally on television. I don't work in front of the camera, I work behind it. So she got me."

—*Danny McNeese, KATV technical director*

"She was great to work with because she wasn't afraid to talk to anybody. When she would get out of the car — I wish more reporters would be like this — she would start asking people for interviews. We would get the story done quickly. That's one thing I miss about her, not everybody was like that. She wasn't afraid of anybody. And when she would talk to them she would treat them like anybody else. She would laugh and smile and that's one thing I liked about her as a reporter because we got the story over with and done and we were ready to go back."

—*Ray Hamilton, KATV photojournalist*

"We did a major promotional shoot with Waymack and Crew using all of our reporters and anchors. It involved 25 shots in three days so we were on a tight schedule. Each person only had one line. That's it. Anne did her's in the newsroom and was scripted to say, '… and when the big story breaks.' I don't know why, but she could never get it right. The inflection was wrong over and over again. I've never seen six words take an hour to get right."

—*Randy Dixon, KATV news director*

"We did a major promotional shoot with Waymack and Crew using all of our reporters and anchors. Each person only had one line. That's it. Anne did her's in the newsroom and was scripted to say, '… and when the big story breaks.' I don't know why, but she could never get it right. I've never seen six words take an hour to get right."
—*Randy Dixon*

Bill Dailey and Anne at the
Purple Hull Pea Festival

"Anne and I loved to cover festivals. With festivals, people are happy to see you there. Often that's not the case with other stories. In June 2005, during a Saturday *Daybreak* show, Anne was the field reporter from the Purple Hull Pea Festival in my hometown of Emerson. The big event there is the World Championship Rotary Tiller Race – a race of souped-up garden tillers. Anne was dressed impeccably in khaki Bermuda shorts and a denim jacket. Nevertheless, she decided to get behind one of the fastest of the garden tillers, and take it for a whirl down the track of plowed ground. Photographer Marcus McDonald got the camera ready and said, 'Go Boo.' What she expected, I don't know. What happened was this: The tiller slung a mighty cloud of dirt clods. Clod after clod was making a direct hit to her body. Some to the midsection, some lower, some higher. A great cloud of dust arose from the earth. Her eyes were squinted; she could have used some goggles. Finally, she let go, the tiller came to a halt and she emerged from the haze. And she was laughing hysterically. We took the tape to the satellite uplink truck, put it in the tape machine, and watched again, this time in slow motion, as one clod after another would make impact to her torso and disintegrate. Beth Hunt would later tell me it was some of the funniest video she'd ever seen. Anne's total lack of pretentiousness was one of her most endearing qualities. This episode, along with so many others, caused her to become one of my favorite people on earth."

—*Bill Dailey, former KATV satellite truck operator*

Anne at the World Championship Rotary Tiller Race

"**A**nne had built this boat ... I still have a picture of her lying down, floating in that ungainly contraption of hers. It's a treasured memory."
—*Bill Dailey*

Anne at the Cardboard Boat Races in Heber Springs

"We found out that *Good Morning America* was coming to West Helena and Anne was like, 'Well, I want to cover that and I'll see what I can do on getting us there.' We thought Robin Roberts would be there and Anne knew I was a big fan of hers and always wanted to meet her. It turned out to be David Muir instead, which we had fun with anyway. But on the way home, she said 'I'm going to find some way that you can meet Robin.' And she ended up coming through of course! Robin Roberts was going to be in Texarkana doing a breast cancer speaking engagement. So after we got finished with a Lake Hamilton pep rally, we ended up going down to Texarkana and meeting Robin Roberts! I thought I had met my hero that day ... but my hero had been in front of me all the time and I just didn't realize it. I really look back at that and smile because Anne was going to make sure that I got to meet Robin Roberts with her."

—*Courtney Dixon, KATV production assistant*

Anne with Robin Roberts (top) and David Muir (above) of ABC News

"In July 2005, I was assigned to do a Saturday *Daybreak* live shot with Anne at the Cardboard Boat Races in Heber Springs. That morning, I left early from the studio in Newstar, the satellite uplink truck, and headed toward Cleburne County. Just before I got to Jacksonville, I received a phone call from photographer Zack McDonald. He asked where I was, and if I could come back to the studio. He explained, 'Anne has built this boat.' It turned out that Anne had been up late the night before, building a cardboard boat of her own in the KATV newsroom. Zack said it was too big to put in his news vehicle, but thought it'd fit nicely in Newstar. Fortunately, I had adequate time, so I turned around in Jacksonville and made my way back to the studio in downtown Little Rock. Upon walking into the newsroom, I saw, in the middle of the floor, this piece of cardboard. Where Anne found it I do not know, but it appeared to have been recently salvaged from a convenient trash bin. There had been some sparse use of duct tape during assembly. To the starboard side of the cardboard boat she had attached white poster board with the Circle 7 and 'KATV' written in blue. Unfortunately, the poster board was too flimsy to remain upright, and it resembled a thin, limp glob of pizza dough. One other thing was readily obvious: There was no way this thing was ever going to float. We carried it down the parking deck ramp, taking extra care given the fragility of the 'boat' and placed it in Newstar. Once in Heber Springs, Anne's plan was to put her creation in the water and actually take a ride during her last live shot of the morning. This concerned us. She was using a wireless microphone. Those things aren't cheap. I told her to hand me the microphone just prior to boarding her self-constructed vessel, and I would hold it close enough so we could still hear her. I assumed we might be able to hear her gurgling. The time came. The lip of her boat might have been 8 inches tall. Anne was something like 5'9" or 5'10". She was about to get in. She was about to sink. But Anne, by swinging her long legs into the boat and sliding the rest of her body in horizontally all at once, managed to not only enter her boat without incident, she then proceeded to maneuver around using a cardboard paddle, another one of her creations. She fooled us all. Eventually I felt comfortable enough to hand the wireless microphone back to her. I had my camera with me that day, and I still have a picture of her lying down, floating in that ungainly contraption of hers. It's a treasured memory."

—*Bill Dailey, former KATV satellite truck operator*

Anne with Wayne Cox at Toad Suck Daze

"Anne was a 'trooper' during Toad Suck Daze each May. She judged the Toad Suck Superstars. She would race toads, but I would say she wasn't crazy about holding the toads. She was always sweet to converse with our friend Vernon Johnson. However, she did beat Vernon in a toad race. (Truth be known, I think Vernon smashed his toad trying to encourage him to move.)"

—*Wayne Cox, KATV sales account executive*

"Once Anne started interning, you thought she had been here several years. It got to the point that guests thought that she would be interviewing them or that she was producing the show. She was able to grab you with a hello and she was able to bring stuff out of you that you didn't know you had. She'd tell you to calm down, this will only be three or four minutes, and she'd put you at ease."

—*Tyrone McIntosh, KATV studio production*

"**H**ere's a memory I have shared with those who have asked what it was like to work with Anne. We were assigned to do a story on Donald Trump visiting northwest Arkansas. Wal-Mart brought him in to speak at a big education-business luncheon. When we checked in at the media counter, we were told there would be no availability for one-on-one interviews with Mr. Trump but we could videotape the speech. We were standing on the camera platform and Anne whispered to me that she knew which door Mr. Trump would enter through. She asked if I would go with her to the front of the ballroom near the door and wait with the camera. Within a couple of minutes, Mr. Trump walked through the door with the Wal-Mart folks. Anne was like a magnet as Trump walked straight over to her. She asked if he had time for an interview and he said he had time for a couple of quick questions. She got the only one-on-one with him after being told that would not be possible."

—Tim Hamilton, KATV chief photojournalist

Anne with Donald Trump

"**W**ell she filled in for Pam Smith on the weekends. Anne was 2 feet taller than me I think (I'm Little Rock's shortest meteorologist). Every time I finished weather, I would go back and sit at the desk on those two black and white pillows so that on camera our heights would equalize out a little bit and look normal on television. That was one of my favorite memories. And one time she wrote down on a piece of paper right there when I came back, 'Coco balls' and I read it and I started laughing and she was laughing."

—Todd Yakoubian, KATV weekend meteorologist

"**I** was impressed with her drive to learn a story and tell it in a professional and unbiased way. She may not have always wanted to do news but she was going to give her best before moving on."

—Stewart McLendon, KATV chief editor

"**A**nne was the new producer of *Good Morning Arkansas*. During one of her first shows there was a live shot that used the services of Newstar, the KATV satellite uplink truck. In order to receive the satellite signal, it's necessary for the video engineer – located in the 'bowels' of Channel 7 – to know several things. These include which satellite, the frequency, and other data. Normally such information is placed on the show's 'run-down' sheet, which is an outline and plan for the program. Anne, being new, failed to include the information for the satellite live shot. As a result, the video engineer wasn't even aware there was going to be a live shot until the director began asking for it. Such moments tend to generate television chaos. Shortly after the show was over, I was in engineering, and saw Anne walk out of the stairwell. She headed directly to video engineering area. She began apologizing profusely to the engineer, explaining how sorry she was for the error. That stuck with me. Not just the fact that she apologized, but the way she did it. She didn't give the engineer a call on the phone; she didn't give a shout over the headset system. She came down to the bowels of Channel 7 and apologized in person. That's when I first suspected she might be someone special."

—Bill Dailey, former KATV satellite truck operator

*"**S**he was smart ... she was funny and had a great time and a great zest for life, and she was a good hard worker..."*
—*Ned Perme*

BEN KRAIN

*Anne and crew before
a staff meeting*

"She was smart. I think a lot of people might not realize that. She was funny and had a great time and a great zest for life, and she was a good hard worker. Boy she could hustle and get some great stories. She knew when to work and she knew when to have fun."

—*Ned Perme, KATV chief meteorologist*

"Anne was a good reporter. She grasped the concept of every story ... she tried very hard to do that. She thought past the surface of the story, rather than just spitting it out. She tried to do a really good piece. Whether it was visually or maybe she was trying to do a really good stand up or if it was just trying to understand the material, the complexity of it and then spit it back out for the public to understand. She was a good reporter. I think she was the first of kind of a wave of us getting some really solid thinkers in the newsroom."

—*Scott Inman, KATV news anchor*

"She was fun to go on stories with, even if it was a story you weren't interested in. She could make it interesting."
—*Mike Herman, KATV photojournalist*

"We spent the 2008 Cotton Bowl together in Dallas. It made my trip to have Anne there, as I, still a Yankee, still felt semi-new to Arkansas and the Razorback culture. Anne, on the other hand, was in her element at an event like the Cotton Bowl. She knew everyone in the hotel, she knew where to go in Dallas and we rang in the new year the night before the New Year's Day game with other Little Rock media people. I will forever remember that trip because Anne was there and the special time we had the chance to share together."

—*Samantha Friedman, Arkansas Democrat Gazette reporter*

"**W**here I thought she would be great ... was the tailgate parties. It's all about capturing the spirit ... and her excitement was perfect..."
—*Steve Sullivan*

Anne at KATV's "We've Got Spirit Pep Rally"

"I always heard stories of her working in the field. Going to tornadoes and changing her clothes in the back seat of photographer's cars and sticking her leg out the window. There was one story where she went to Marmaduke to cover a tornado. They had driven all night and I remember her telling me that she and the photographer went into a small school to use the bathroom. She went into the women's restroom and he went into the men's restroom. The photographer realized there was no electricity in there and so he started knocking on the women's restroom door. He said 'Anne, do you have power?' And she said, 'Yeah, come on in!' because she apparently had a candle in that bathroom. So the photographer and Anne went in there and did their thing and came back with just a funny story. She would say 'Hey, we peed together in Marmaduke, we bonded.' And that's just one of the crazy things that Anne would do."

—*Angela Rachels, KATV assignment editor*

"Where I thought she would be great, and actually probably one of her last assignments, was the tailgate parties. It's all about capturing the spirit ... and her excitement was perfect. You don't really have to know anything about the game, just the atmosphere. She did a great job bringing that out. Actually if you look back to the clips, she was at her best when she went to places like Rison and was with the Hedge Dwellers. I really didn't think anyone could follow Jason Harper and do as good of job as Jason Harper but she did, you know even better than he did, and I'd tell that to Jason."

—*Steve Sullivan, KATV sports director*

32 *Making Memories*

KATV News Director Randy Dixon and Anne as featured in High Profile

AFTER HOURS

Anne was all about making memories. No matter what! It didn't matter if she had worked a 14-hour day and had to be up early the next morning, she'd find time to make a memory. Anne was always entertaining others. Television personalities are often asked to be a part of events or fundraisers and Anne loved that part of her job. Not only would she volunteer her time, she'd put so much effort into making the event the best it could be.

"One of her favorite events was the Symphony Designer House. I had tickets and we stopped by after work one day. They put a flower on my lapel and boa around her neck. Phyllis Brandon of [Arkansas Democrat Gazette's] 'High Profile' stopped us for a picture. You have to understand that Anne was pretty tall and I'm not. We posed and Phyllis said, 'Wait, Randy, you need to be taller and Anne, honey, you need to be shorter.' So, I stood on my tiptoes and she hunched downed for the picture. It was kind of embarrassing at the time, but we got our picture in 'High Profile' and I look tall."

—Randy Dixon, KATV news director

"I like to say that Anne saved my life ... and she liked to say that, too. It was during the infamous I-30 speedway races, the golf cart race. Anne and I were not doing so well. We got sabotaged by another station and we ran onto an embankment. I flew out of the cart and all of a sudden Anne left the cart, reached over, grabbed me and pulled me back. So we laughed about that for a long time. We had a fun night and kind of made that our little tradition. We did it again the next year but did it a little better. So yeah, that's one of my favorite memories ... Anne the lifesaver!"

—Amanda Manatt, KATV reporter

Anne and Ned Perme with the KATV Celebrity Karaoke cheerleaders

DeWAINE DUNCAN

"Anne was kind of the head honcho of the Celebrity Karaoke. It was her team sport of sports. We were going to do 'Hey Mickey' and we were all going to be cheerleaders and this required a fair amount of athleticism and coordination on our part and intense choreography. She was hot gluing hair bows and was right in the middle of it. She and Christina kind of spearheaded this and she was a drill sergeant. You had to be at the practices and if you weren't she didn't like that at all. And I mean we were tired. We had been flipping over backwards. We had been lifting people up in the air. I was working *Nightside* at the time so I would work and leave on my dinner break and then come back and I was just really tired. So then one night she said, '[Jason] Pederson has found this karaoke restaurant or karaoke club at the Howard Johnson's in North Little Rock,' and she said we all need to go practice there. She calls me and I think I had applied self tanner and smelled like it. She said, 'Okay, I'm coming to get you.' I was like, 'Anne it's 10:45 on a Wednesday night and I'm just really tired.' She said, 'Well we're all tired, you're coming!' I'm like, 'What?,' then I hear beep, beep and she's sitting out there with her lights on. I hear my phone ring and it's Heather Crawford, 'Jess, I'm out here in the car with Anne. She kidnapped me. Please come out here so we can go and I can go home please.' So, I was like all right fine. I put my clothes on and I get out there and get in the back seat of the car. I shut the door and I say, 'Okay, I'm here, let's go.' She puts the car in park and turns around to me and says, 'We're making a memory, you'll thank me later,' throws it in reverse and off we went. We get to this place and it is just a ridiculously smoky, old karaoke bar that has a really random assortment of people and here we are taking Christina Muñoz, throwing her in the air and the entire time we just start laughing and it turns out to be this wildly fun night. Anne just kept going, 'You're making a memory, you're making a memory, you can thank me later.' And, of course we all do now because we hold those memories very close. When she had something in her mind, it was going to happen; you were going to be there whether you wanted to or not."

—*Jessica Dean, KATV reporter*

"She was fearless. We always do Christmas karaoke where we invite the local anchors to come in and sing for charity. One time, we were short and I needed some filler so I went to all the Channel 7 girls and asked, 'Would anybody be willing to sing to fill some time?' Nobody would do it except for Anne. Anne said, 'I'll do it on one condition … if you go up there with me.' Anne wasn't the best singer but she got up there in front of all those people and I'll never forget that. She was fearless."

—David Bazzel, 103.7 The Buzz radio host

Anne with David Bazzel

"I'm real self-conscious. I won't do something if I'm not somewhat capable of doing it. But the great thing I liked about Anne is that regardless of what she did, she would just do it. For instance, when she played in the Buzz flag football game … she was very concerned about how she looked for the event. She would go to the point where she would buy the right shorts and the socks and she'd look like the star player. She may not perform, but she'd bring great spirit to the game and always had the idea. I remember when she did the cardboard boat race and most people would just show up and do something, but I think she stayed up all night building the boat for the race. That was Anne to a T."

—Steve Sullivan, KATV sports director

"Anne loved to dance and loved to choreograph our Christmas karaoke charity event. Every year she always played a big role in it. The year that we did 'Hey Mickey' and dressed up in cheerleading uniforms, Anne made sure everyone had everything down pat and had so much fun choreographing it. I remember there was one night probably about a week before the performance and she said, 'Come on we've got to go practice, they're having karaoke night at a local hotel.' I didn't want to go, I had no desire to do karaoke in front of a bunch of strangers but she said, 'Come on, we're going to go make memories!' That's how she was. She lived life to the fullest. She always was about making memories and enjoying her life."

—Heather Crawford, KATV anchor/reporter

"When I first told Anne that I was pregnant, she said, "When's your due date?" I told her it was in October and she said "Oh good, so you can be back in shape by December for Celebrity Karaoke!"

—Christina Muñoz, KATV news anchor

Jessica Dean, Amanda Manatt, Anne, Christina Muñoz and Shilo Groover Korzen singing karaoke

"I remember when we were at Classics singing karaoke as a group and she sang 'Fancy.' I was just blown away by how good it was. I mean, I knew Anne could sing because she would sing pop songs around the newsroom, and I'd sing pop songs around the newsroom. We had the same taste in music, had the same humor, but she really sang it and I was just floored by how good it was. I thought it was a fitting tribute when they performed that in her honor at the last Christmas karaoke because she could really sing that song."

—Jason Pederson, KATV consumer reporter

"I am grateful for the many times Anne and I chuckled ourselves out of our seats. Like the times we set out to play flag football — that's when we became "T-N-A" — and as only Tomeca & Anne would do, we made game-day shorts with our new 'logo.' Of course, we were often no-shows at practice and when we did attend, it became the perfect set-up for our cartwheel competition. Nevertheless, we filled the empty positions on the team's roster and we were darn cute doing it. Then ... there was a time we actually REHEARSED for a colleague's karaoke party. Yep, we became the best Whitney Houstons we could be. That performance was complete with a blue wig and choreographed dance."

—*Tomeca Sloan, former KATV producer*

*Anne with
Tomeca Sloan*

"We'll never do Celebrity Karaoke and not think of Anne. The very first year we did it, it wasn't anything like it is now. It was just the guys at the Buzz calling us and just going, 'Hey come sing something,' It was just in fun. Well that morning it was just me, Beth and, I think, Christina, so mainly the anchors were going to go do it. And of course, if it meant singing, dancing and on stage, Anne was not going to be left out! She's like, 'I'm going to go, too.' So we get there and were all worried about what song we're going to sing. You know, is it going too be to high? Is it going to be too low? Anne wanted to do the Pussy Cat Dolls one ... 'Don't Cha Wish Your Girlfriend Was Hot Like Me.' Well that was too new and so they didn't have it in the system. She gets up there and she picks Shania Twain's song 'Any Man of Mine' and she gets up there and she's not worried about a thing. She does these dance moves that she remembers from high school. When she started the screen said key of B or something like that or B flat and she reads that and goes 'I don't know what that means, but I'm gonna go ahead and sing, ya'll.' Everybody just loved her, you know? And Celebrity Karaoke just grew and grew and she was just a big part of that."

—*Melinda Mayo, KATV meteorologist*

"Anne signed the board in October of last year. She co-hosted a show with me for my birthday. She put a stick figure up there with a #53, the Buzz and 'love ya, mean it!' It's still there today."

—*David Bazzel, 103.7 The Buzz radio host*

"Her signature is still up in the studio from the last time she was up here."
—*Tommy Smith, 103.7 The Buzz radio host*

Back row, left to right: Michelle Rupp, Anne, Jessica Morkert, Kristin Fisher, Beth Hunt; front row, left to right: Melinda Mayo and Christina Muñoz performing at Celebrity Karaoke

"I spent the most time with Anne around Christmastime when we'd be gearing up for Celebrity Karaoke. The first year, we both got up on a little stage and sang solos. (She admittedly didn't sound great, but didn't care because she had so much fun dancing!) But the second year, Anne decided that we should go all out. And boy did we!! She had this crazy idea that we should do the song 'Hey Mickey' and that we all would be wearing cheerleading outfits. I was a little leery of the idea at first and thought it might be too silly. But Anne persisted. Before I knew it, we were meeting at a dance studio every chance we got so we could choreograph a routine for the Channel 7 girls. She had been a cheerleader, and I had been a dancer so we made a great team. Other dancers at the studio would see us acting so goofy and peek their heads in. I always felt a little embarrassed working so hard on something so silly ... but Anne loved it! She'd invite everyone in and say, 'Check this out!' or 'what do you think of this?' Then we had to teach the routine to the Channel 7 girls. Anne became known as the 'Dance Nazi!' She worked the girls so hard! AND made us do back flips and big lifts! It was really crazy. I couldn't believe all the things she wanted us to do. But somehow she pulled it off. Then, the night before the performance she stayed up almost all night making little hair bows for each of us. What a trooper! We ended up in second place ... but with memories that will last a lifetime.

—*Christina Muñoz, KATV news anchor*

"Another favorite Anne memory would have to be the infamous LL Cool J concert at Riverfest 2007. It's hot. We're all tired. But Anne is determined to make a memory. She is going to get on that stage and she's going to drag all of us up there with her. There is no way any of us are getting out of it, and we know it. Anne works her way to the front of the stage, gets LL Cool J's attention in two seconds and before you know it, the entire KATV crew is getting down on center stage with LL Cool J. It was quite a moment. Anne, thank you. It was something I never would have dreamed of doing, but it ended up being one of my favorite memories of all time."

—*Kristin Fisher, former KATV reporter*

SHOWBIZ

Anne's life could have been that of a movie script. There was always something unique or dramatic going on. Hardly a day would pass without Anne telling of some bizarre experience she'd had. As much as she kept up with current news, she was even more in-the-know about celebrities, movies, and pop stars. She was the epitome of cool and hip. And the rest of us were a little cooler and a little hipper just by being around her.

One of Anne's favorite pictures was an Andy Warhol-inspired treatment Randy Dixon did while he was learning Photoshop

"It was almost like her life was set to a musical. There was always a song in her head, a song in her heart and she was always running around singing."

—*Melinda Mayo, KATV meteorologist*

"I had the pleasure of going with Anne to the premiere of the movie and it was so funny because all of us were bugging her about finding out if she was in it. She kept saying, 'I don't think I'm going to be in it, I don't think I'm going to be in it.' But knowing Anne and her personality, you knew it was a done deal. And so we went to the premiere. Everybody got there early except for Anne ... she was the last one to arrive. But it was fun because a lot of people had brought flowers and stuff to congratulate her. She was really excited and that was a pretty memorable experience. And then she fell asleep. I think she was so tired after having a long day she fell asleep during the movie and somebody had to wake her up!"

—*Pamela Smith, KATV weekend anchor*

"One of the last projects I did with her had nothing to do with TV. It was a photo shoot. KATV always sponsors the American Heart Association Wine Festival in October and I donate a framed photo for the silent auction. They asked that all of the items that year be wine-themed. Anne agreed to be the "model" for a bunch of pictures I took at Acadia Restaurant right before the festival. The pictures were great, but she was uncomfortable with some of them because she was holding a glass of wine and she didn't even drink. So we decided to use one that you only see her eyes out of focus behind some wine bottles. No one even knew it was her in the photo."

—*Randy Dixon, KATV news director*

"I used to tease her a lot about a magazine called *Soiree*. She was always in it. This one time she wasn't in it and I told her she was slipping, I said, 'You're not in *Soiree* this month what happened?' She said she just didn't make the cut this month. She was always a lot of fun."

—*Mike Herman, KATV photojournalist*

"If she had a weakness, it was for gossip or celebrity mags. She had three or four. She knew what was going on in every Hollywood person's life. If you wanted to know how to pronounce a name of someone in Hollywood, you just asked Anne and she would know that stuff. She made it fun; she had a fun time keeping up with that stuff. I think she could have been a entertainment reporter. I mean I think she was a great reporter, but I think her sweet spot might have been entertainment reporting if she had gone that route. She really enjoyed that, she just enjoyed life."

—*Jason Pederson, KATV consumer reporter*

*Melissa Dunbar-Gates
and Anne in LA
(Louisiana)*

*Anne and crew with Dixie
Carter and Hal Holbrook*

*Melissa, Josh Brolin
and Anne*

Anne and Oliver Stone

"One of the things I remember the most was when she was in that movie 'W.' The weekend it was opening her mother was coming in and her friends were here and I said, 'Do you want to have an opportunity to watch the movie before anyone else?' because she didn't get to go to the premiere. So we had a show just for her and I and maybe one other person and watched the movie. It was really funny because when she saw herself on the movie she didn't recognize herself. I said, 'Anne it's you,' and I have no idea of what it's like to see yourself on the big screen but it may be overwhelming you know, I said, 'That's you, Anne,' and she was so giddy. You're in a movie theatre and it's cold and I still have the sweatshirt jacket that I gave her to wear and there are things about that day and after that I remember. After the movie, I introduced her to my friend who was the theater manager. They had roped off a couple of rows for her and had signs on the seats for her and it was kind of like her red carpet. She was so thankful and so happy because it was a big deal to her and that's always going to be my best memory of Anne."

—*Danny-Joe Crofford, 103.7 The Buzz producer*

"Anne was a true Southern lady. She looked up to and admired other Southern belles who'd made a name for themselves. I happened to be with Anne on what had to be one of the happiest days of her life! If you knew Anne, you knew that she was a huge fan of the TV program Designing Women. One of the program's stars Dixie Carter came to town for a speaking engagement, and our News Director Randy Dixon got us tickets to the event and a chance to personally meet Ms. Carter and her husband Hal Holbrook. Several of us crowded into a back room at Baptist Medical Center in Little Rock to meet the celebrities; and when they came in, Anne perked up like a kid on Christmas morning. After some small talk and photos, Anne started reciting lines and details from scenes of Designing Women to Dixie. Because she had watched every episode several times, she was an expert on the dialogue. Ms. Carter was obviously impressed. She said, 'You really are a fan. I didn't even remember that scene.' It obviously made Anne very happy that she had made such an impression and connection with one of her favorite stars. I was just glad that I was there to witness such a joyous time in Anne's life-- the day she met Dixie and Hal -or should I say Julia and Reese."

—*Rusty Mizell, KATV assistant news director*

"I remember her unbelievable energy. I credit Anne with keeping an old guy like me up on pop culture. She would come in the newsroom singing (always) and it could have been Fergie, Eminem, Lady Gaga, Pink or Neil Diamond. I knew only Neil until Anne came onto the scene. The newsroom and our lives could only be less fun, less interesting, less joyous without Anne. She is irreplaceable."

—*Barry Brandt, KATV meteorologist*

"Only Anne could be working on a news story and end up with a role in a movie! She was sent to Shreveport to do a story on the tax incentive package Louisiana offers filmmakers. The casting director she interviewed told her she could be an "Ann Coulter" look-alike. Anne wasn't sure if that was a compliment or not but the casting director explained that she was looking for someone to play an "Ann Coulter" character for an upcoming movie. Anne thought she was joking but the casting director convinced her to audition for the role. Anne had done some acting in the past, including a bit part on a soap opera, and decided to go for it. Well, it turns out this wasn't just any movie... it was Oliver Stone's movie about George W Bush's presidency called "W"! Not only did she get the part, but then Oliver Stone asked her to ad lib some lines and if she could make him laugh...he said he'd add them to the movie. Well, of course, she made him laugh! It sounded like she made everyone on the movie set laugh! That's just the way Anne was. Whether she was in the presence of friends or big-time filmmakers like Oliver Stone."

— *Christina Muñoz, KATV news anchor*

Christina Muñoz, Anne, Jessica Dean, Brian Ferguson, Heather Crawford, Jason Pederson at a practice for the December 2007 Celebrity Karaoke

"The movie came out on Friday and I talked to her Friday and we were just waiting, waiting and waiting, is this going to happen? She would call B 98 and give us updates. It's funny when she would hang up from those updates people would say it's like listening to a younger Lisa Fischer because she would just talk, talk, talk. My co-host would go, 'All right we're up against the news, we gotta go' and she would go, 'All right, love ya, bye.' That Friday she sent me a text, it may have been a mass text sent to everybody, but it just said 'In.' She went at 2:00 and saw it and so I wrote back 'shut up,' and she wrote back 'not kidding.' It was just so Anne. It just made me laugh."

—Lisa Fischer, B98 radio host

"She seemed to LOVE celebrity gossip magazines! In fact, she had a whole stack of them on her desk — 'US Weekly,' 'In Touch,' 'People' even 'Ok Magazine.' Now, walking into a number-one rated newsroom with renowned journalistic integrity, I didn't want to admit that I buy one of these gossip magazines at least once a week; but seeing Anne vigorously thumbing through the latest on Martha Stewart insider secrets, Jude Law's affair with his nanny — you get the idea — most girls can't help but take part in the mayhem. The tradition would carry on when Anne became a reporter. Every Friday we would go into the morning meeting and afterwards, Anne would pull out a stack of the latest celebrity gossip. So, while lots of reporters might be furiously trying to track down some politician about the latest scandal, on Fridays, at Channel 7 — the girls in the newsroom with Anne at the helm, were learning about Fergie's relationship with Josh Duhamel. Of course, not everyone can appreciate the entertainment value of 'Trashy Magazine Fridays.' After about an hour of Anne's trademark loud laugh – we would get the evil eye from the bosses. 'Girls would you keep it down, some people are trying to put together a news show,' Rusty Mizell would say. 'Anne, don't make me have to come split you up. Use your inside voice. Y'all are like little school girls,' Alan Faulkner would say. But telling a group of 20-something girls to quiet down only adds fuel to the fire. There would be many adolescent moments in the newsroom from then on."

—Jessica Morkert, former KATV reporter

FUN, FOOD AND DIET COKE

If Anne had any vices, they would be high fashion, junk food and Diet Cokes. No one is quite sure how many colas she consumed in a day, but there was surely one close by. Her enviable metabolism allowed her to eat almost anything and maintain a fit figure without ever working out. Anne always looked perfect. She was able to maintain a high fashion look on a low dollar budget-- a bit like Fifth Avenue meets Main Street. Whether she was in business attire for a newscast, a gown at a fundraising event or a ball cap covering a tornado, Anne was stylish and gorgeous.

"There was this drive-thru not in business anymore called Fazoli's where you could get Italian food. She liked it and Michelle Rupp liked it and we always used to talk about it. It went out of business one day. I was talking to her and Michelle and I said if this TV thing doesn't work out we could open Fazoli's. I could be the cook and Michelle could work the dining room and Anne could work the drive-thru window. It was just nonsense like that, that was so much fun. I just thought that she was fun — never too serious."

—Mike Herman, KATV photojournalist

"She was very generous when she would buy candy at the store. She would buy like four bags of candy and bring them back and just open them up at the same time and say, 'Hey candy at my desk.' I was always thankful for that because I usually needed a sugar high at about 3:30 and she could provide that."

—Jason Pederson, KATV consumer reporter

"When Anne was an intern we needed a segment for the next day. We were short one guest over at *Good Morning Arkansas*. Christy McWilliams was the producer at the time and she said, 'You know, I don't have anyone to fill this hole in my show.' Anne overheard this in the newsroom and she said, 'I'll do a segment.' Christy said, 'Well what are you going to do?' and she said, 'We'll make some clothes or something.' So Anne went and figured out how to take t-shirts and cut them up and did this segment and it was just wonderful. I mean it was so Anne. Later I laughed and thought you know I never saw Anne actually wear any of the clothes she made but just on a moment's notice she made this segment great on how to make clothes."

—*Melinda Mayo, KATV meteorologist*

"Christian. Friend. Beautiful. Hilarious. Talented. These are just a few words that come to mind when I think about Anne Pressly. She was a loyal friend and a burst of sunshine in all of our lives. What I remember most is her passion for God and for life, oh, and let's not forget, she loved Diet Coke!"

—*Sandra Kirk, KLRT reporter*

"Anne had an unbelievable fashion sense. She was extremely talented in being able to create things at home, to create something out of nothing. Whether it was fabric or a boa, decorating a picture frame, she was just very, I mean we're all to some degree artistic, but she took it a little bit further. And she just could always add that pizzazz to that homemade object that set it apart. You would have thought, 'Oh my gosh how much was that? 30 40 50 bucks? No I just made it last night.' We would say you made that? And that was one of her many talents — that she could literally take someone else's trash and turn it into a treasure."

—*Michelle Rupp, KATV reporter*

"When she finally became a reporter, it was like a new chapter in KATV history. The newsroom lit up! It didn't matter what time of day Anne showed up to work. It was always, 'Hey y'all. I'm here' ... and boy was she. No matter how serious the mood or intense the deadline, Anne could make you smile. She was the absolute 'Queen of Fashion.' Whether heading to the State Capitol or covering one of the many festivals in Arkansas, she was dressed to the nines. She filled in for me a couple of times on live shots. One time in particular, she had to get dirty on a farm. She showed up in Prada leather boots and her Gucci sunglasses. Everyone was dying laughing. It was like an episode from 'Green Acres.' "

—*Jason Harper, former KATV morning host*

"She was the one person who cared if you got a new pair of fabulous shoes and just wanted to show someone, or you had the courage to paint your nails some funky purple color ... she was as excited about it as you were. If it mattered to you, it mattered to Anne."

—*Melinda Mayo, KATV meteorologist*

"She was the one person who cared ... If it mattered to you, it mattered to Anne."
—Melinda Mayo

Anne preps for a promotional shoot for KATV

"One of my favorite memories of Anne involves one of her true loves — fashion. Dolly Parton was going to be in Little Rock, and we thought it would be a blast. Amanda Manatt, Kate Sullivan and Rusty Jackson were going as well. We got our tickets, and Anne put together a Dolly mix CD for us to prepare for the show. I'm not sure where the idea came from, but she also wanted to make us all matching T-shirts to wear to the concert. Someone came up with the phrase 'Dolly or Bust' ... and the rest is history."

—Amanda Kelton, former KATV producer

"She would say or we would always say, 'Fake looks good on us.' She would put the track on her hair or weave and I would put my fake hair in, fake eyelashes, fake tan. When you're 46 you're fake from the shoulders down sometimes. I'm just saying, you know, it happens. And that's just something she would always say, 'Fake looks good on us.' You know if all else fails, if things are looking bad, she said I could always slap on a little lipstick, a little nail polish, put my fake hair in and I'm out the door."

—Lisa Fischer, B98 radio host

Melissa Dunbar-Gates and Anne

"My favorite story about Anne took place when we were in San Antonio together just months before she was attacked. She had convinced me we HAD to attend a Beth Moore conference. It turned out to be one of the best weekends of my life. I'm forever grateful for the peace I feel from things we did and learned at the conference. But the best part of the weekend came when Anne walked out of the bathroom one morning after just having taken a shower clutching to a 20-ounce Diet Coke that was dripping wet. It was so obvious Anne had just taken a shower with that soda. I immediately asked her what was up with that and she admitted to having placed the Diet Coke on the ledge inside the shower. Her explanation was great, 'What if I get light-headed during my shower and need a sip?' It would be right there at her fingertips, of course. How silly of me to not have thought of that! No, the soda wasn't propped up on the bathroom sink still within reach of the shower, it was actually IN the shower with her. I love that SO much. I can not pick up a 20-ounce Diet Coke without imagining it in the shower!"

—Melissa Dunbar-Gates, KTHV reporter

"When it was announced that George Strait was going to be in town we were even more excited. Of course Anne went to work designing a shirt. That girl could make a white T-shirt into a ball gown if she had to. She was constantly making or decorating something. We could walk into Target, and walk out 30 minutes later with a complete new outfit ... head to toe ... and all on sale. Nobody could bargain shop like that girl."

—Amanda Kelton, former KATV producer

"The fun times and memories kept on coming! From the Dixie Cafe fried pickle lunches to Route 44's at Sonic and the numerous reminders that we needed to 'get to work' ... not only were our work desks connected, but often our silly thoughts were quite connected as well."

—*Tomeca Sloan, former KATV producer*

"I think Anne could have lived on Chick-fil-A. Her favorites were the breakfast chicken minis. She was convinced that the secret ingredients in them were love and crack."

—*Randy Dixon, KATV news director*

"She loved sushi, and we shared many a good after-work conversation over sushi."

—*Samantha Friedman, Arkansas Democrat Gazette reporter*

Anne and Randy Dixon at a colleague's wedding reception

"So we would be at El Porton restaurant solving the world's problems and I have a photograph when we went to El Porton in August of 2007. Her mom was here and it was the three of us and Shiloh showed up and they brought out the big sombrero and all of the staff at El Porton would recognize us because literally we were there almost every Monday night. Her last week here she said, 'Shelley we've got to schedule another El Porton.' Her schedule had changed and we hadn't seen each other in a while and we just needed that, we just needed to reconnect so we needed to go to El Porton. I remember going, 'Annie you name it, you tell me when's good for you and I'm there.' So that was a very special place for the two of us. That was our restaurant. Probably everybody has a restaurant with Anne because she loved food and she loved Diet Coke. She did not go anywhere without one. She and Kate and I were in Dallas and she took her Diet Coke with her into the shower, in case she felt faint she would have her Diet Coke there with her. I had never, never seen anything like it before. But that's part of what made Anne so unique, that's her."

—*Michelle Rupp, KATV reporter*

Anne at El Porton restaurant

Anne loved designer handbags. Shown here are black and white "portraits" of her two favorite labels

Melissa Dunbar-Gates and Anne

"Anne had a fondness for expensive purses. On a reporter's salary, she couldn't really afford them but she did have a couple: a Prada and a Louis Vuitton. As a matter of fact, I think she even leased one of them. She found a website where you could "rent to own" a designer purse. As a joke, I matted and framed black and white "portraits" of her two favorite handbags. I was surprised that she actually loved the pictures and hung them in her living room."

—Randy Dixon, KATV news director

"I loved her shoes. She had the best shoe collection ever. And people always, well they used to tease me, I don't buy shoes as much now — they used to say, 'Oh you have the best shoes.' I think Anne had me beat. She had probably a pair of shoes for every single outfit. She had this really unique way of being able to put together clothing and accessories at great prices. I would ask her, 'Anne where did you get that?' and it would be some place you wouldn't remotely think of shopping. But when she put it on she looked like a million bucks."

—Pamela Smith, KATV weekend anchor

"On my first trip to New York City, I wanted to get a Louis Vuitton and was going to a particular location to acquire a Louis Vuitton handbag. She had flash cards made up so we could spot good quality imitation Louis Vuitton handbags. And I believe it was her senior year at Rhodes, she was in an art class and she painted a Louis Vuitton handbag and I have that at home. When she came back she was like, 'Here this is for you' and it's a Louis Vuitton bag and it's hysterical because it looks just like a Louis Vuitton bag like hers that was one of her favorites."

—Michelle Rupp, KATV reporter

"She talked all the time, and she wanted that interaction with other people. She always wanted to keep going and be busy, busy, busy and when things got quiet it always made her nervous. I remember when she switched to the morning shift, I don't think she realized how quiet it is in the mornings because nobody is here. We're all just kind of typing on our computers and one morning it was just quiet and the scanners weren't really even going, and she stood up and said, 'I can't take it anymore. It's too quiet in here; it's making me nervous. I'm going to Sonic to get a Diet Coke; does anybody want anything?' So she just had to get out because it was too quiet."

—Beth Hunt, KATV morning anchor

"The newsroom was never dull (or quiet … can't tell you how many times Rusty had to shush us … ha) when Anne was there. We bonded over celebrity gossip and Diet Coke."

—Amanda Kelton, former KATV producer

Anne's shoe wardrobe

"I loved her shoes. She had the best shoe collection ever. And people always used to say, 'Oh you have the best shoes.' I think Anne had me beat. She probably had a pair of shoes for every single outfit..."
—*Pamela Smith*

FACEBOOK

"Anne loved facebook. She and Heather Crawford got me to join. I didn't want to at first, because I told Anne, 'I don't want to be that old creepy guy on Facebook.' She said, 'Oh no, that's MySpace. You'd be the creepy old guy on that. There are a lot of old guys on Facebook. Anyway, Myspace is so last year.'"

—*Randy Dixon, KATV news director*

Below are Anne's Facebook postings from the day she joined Facebook, in reverse order.

OCTOBER 19, 2008 AT 9:51PM
ANNE PRESSLY is so thankful for the wonderful friends who came to see my little 30 sec part in *"W."* I'm really behind on my facebooking, y'all. Promise to catch up soon.

OCTOBER 16, 2008 AT 9:29AM
ANNE PRESSLY changed the location of the *"W"* premiere. Now at Breckenridge at 6:50. Thanks, Crofford!

OCTOBER 15, 2008 AT 5:24PM
ANNE PRESSLY would love for y'all to come see *"W"* with me on opening night. 7:15 Friday at The Rave.

OCTOBER 13, 2008 AT 8:38PM
ANNE PRESSLY thinks *"Samantha Who"* might just be the greatest show currently on tv.

OCTOBER 13, 2008 AT 6:56AM
ANNE PRESSLY is sad for Pederson that his pager is broken. Yep, he's got one.

OCTOBER 13, 2008 AT 6:56AM
ANNE PRESSLY is at the longest football game evah. Still tied.

OCTOBER 11, 2008 AT 8:19PM
ANNE PRESSLY is putting together a Race for the Cure mixtape--I mean CD--for Melinda's walkman.

"**A**nne was so friendly and easy to talk to. She really made me feel a part of the group from the word go. She always had a way of making you feel like she really cared about what was going on in your life."
—*Cassie Nicholson*

OCTOBER 11, 2008 AT 1:32 AM
ANNE PRESSLY is loving Clement's status updates. What it do, Clem?

OCTOBER 8, 2008 AT 7:33AM
ANNE PRESSLY is unhappy that the drink machine in the basement gave me a Sprite instead of a Diet Coke.

OCTOBER 7, 2008 AT 8:25AM
ANNE PRESSLY is listening to Clementine bark at a tennis ball while Daisy sleeps. Why can't both dogs behave at the same time??

OCTOBER 5, 2008 AT 6:54PM
ANNE PRESSLY is in Heber waiting for MDG to cross the finish line!

OCTOBER 5, 2008 AT 9:34AM
ANNE PRESSLY is purchasing Christmas music on itunes. Got to start early.

OCTOBER 4, 2008 AT 4:03PM
ANNE PRESSLY is WOW! This is HUGE! Melinda Mayo is on the fbook. Friend her, y'all.

OCTOBER 2, 2008 AT 7:55AM
ANNE PRESSLY is at the new Panera. From here, I'm Motown bound. (Morrilton, not Detroit, natch.)

SEPTEMBER 30, 2008 AT 8:25AM
ANNE PRESSLY just got a shot in the behind!

September 29, 2008 at 5:52pm

ANNE PRESSLY is 6 day work week w/12 hour days...trips to Monticello, Hot Springs, Jonesboro, and Magnolia...plus early morning wake-ups. Pass me a Diet Coke, please

September 28, 2008 at 4:01pm

ANNE PRESSLY is pretty much worthless tonight. And totally ok with it!

September 26, 2008 at 9:27pm

ANNE PRESSLY seconds Beth. David Muir is hot-to-go!

September 25, 2008 at 8:06am

ANNE PRESSLY is in Helena-West Helena for *Good Morning America*!

September 25, 2008 at 6:13am

ANNE PRESSLY is in need of a nap. Ain't gonna happen.

September 24, 2008 at 2:50pm

ANNE PRESSLY is trying to write a news story for tomorrow's *Daybreak*. I can finally get work done now that I know what Jeff is doing!

September 24, 2008 at 7:30am

ANNE PRESSLY is eating a Hot Pocket with Cameron's fork. Thanks, Beth :)

September 24, 2008 at 4:14am

ANNE PRESSLY is "luck is from Harry Potter, blessings come from the Lord"--Marcus McDonald.

September 19, 2008 at 3:56am

ANNE PRESSLY is getting pumped for tomorrow morning's pep rally in Stuttgart...YAY Ricebirds!

September 18, 2008 at 6:02pm

ANNE PRESSLY is eating biscuits and gravy that Melinda brought back from Homer's...yum!

September 18, 2008 at 7:46am

ANNE PRESSLY can't believe Morkert updated her own status...and everything is spelled correctly! YAY, Jess!

September 18, 2008 at 5:29am

ANNE PRESSLY is getting her hair did.

September 17, 2008 at 2:43pm

ANNE PRESSLY is missing her favorite mullet.

September 15, 2008 at 5:16pm

ANNE PRESSLY is getting ready to head to the Old State House Museum for some Sparkle and Twang.

September 15, 2008 at 7:46am

ANNE PRESSLY is thinking this must be what pneumonia is like. However you spell it. Don't feel up to googling it!

September 14, 2008 at 6:16pm

ANNE PRESSLY is s-i-c-k...but working anyway! On my 3rd Diet Coke. Not a good sign!

September 10, 2008 at 5:06am

ANNE PRESSLY is Viva la Vida...

September 8, 2008 at 8:48am

ANNE PRESSLY is beyond offended by the VMA's.

September 7, 2008 at 8:13pm
ANNE PRESSLY is hoping the rumors that Britney will perform at the VMA's are true! It's tradition, for crying out loud!

September 5, 2008 at 10:01pm
ANNE PRESSLY is way excited about the "We've Got Spirit" pep rally tomorrow morning on *Daybreak*!

September 4, 2008 at 9:49pm
ANNE PRESSLY Is seriously wondering whether Entergy crews can be bribed into coming to this street next. It's getting hot up in here. Can't spend my off day without AC!

September 4, 2008 at 5:28am
ANNE PRESSLY is hoping chicken minis from Chick-fil-A will make the electricity-free morning a little better.

September 3, 2008 at 8:35am
ANNE PRESSLY wants the folks at Fox 16 to know that you do weather cut-ins during commercial breaks. Not during the premiere of 90210.

September 2, 2008 at 7:20pm
ANNE PRESSLY is awake. Ish. And counting down until 90210 2.0...party at the Peach Pit!

September 2, 2008 at 3:25am
ANNE PRESSLY now has an AR driver's license. Yikes! Hung onto the SC one for as long as legally allowed.

August 29, 2008 at 5:34pm
ANNE PRESSLY is thankful for the b-day wishes. Love all y'all, mean it!

August 28, 2008 at 8:02am
ANNE PRESSLY wants to stay 25.

August 27, 2008 at 11:40am
ANNE PRESSLY thinks that pickle-o's from Sonic + ranch = heaven. But I'm still praying Sonic will bring back Macaroni Bites.

August 26, 2008 at 3:14pm
ANNE PRESSLY is at the Alamodome!

August 22, 2008 at 6:41pm
ANNE PRESSLY is waiting on lost luggage at the San Antonio airport.

August 22, 2008 at 4:00pm
ANNE PRESSLY is packing...

August 22, 2008 at 6:24am
ANNE PRESSLY is at the Extreme Makeover house! Yay!

August 21, 2008 at 9:17am
ANNE PRESSLY was just asked by some lady in Cabot if I'd put her dead two-headed cat on tv.

August 19, 2008 at 1:22pm
ANNE PRESSLY is trying to figure out Olympic tiebreakers. Why the judges gotta be hatin' on the USA??

August 18, 2008 at 10:13pm
ANNE PRESSLY 's days and nights are officially confused.

August 17, 2008 at 12:33pm

ANNE PRESSLY is making it happen on very little shut-eye!

August 13, 2008 at 10:14pm

ANNE PRESSLY is having trouble winding down. And I have to wake up at 2:45.

August 13, 2008 at 10:14pm

ANNE PRESSLY was just on CNN.

August 13, 2008 at 1:14pm

ANNE PRESSLY is in Conway w/a growling stomach.

August 12, 2008 at 9:04am

ANNE PRESSLY is convinced she has seen Lauren Simpson's pic on Perez....there's just nothing bigger or better than than that!

August 8, 2008 at 8:36am

ANNE PRESSLY is convinced she has seen Lauren Simpson's pic on Perez....there's just nothing bigger or better than than that!

August 7, 2008 at 11:58am

ANNE PRESSLY is at Sonic. It's not even happy hour! Got to have a Route 44 Diet Coke.

August 7, 2008 at 11:58am

ANNE PRESSLY 's entire neighborhood is without power. It's a brownout, apparently. Does this mean global warming is for real?

August 4, 2008 at 12:29am

ANNE PRESSLY is workin'. Sort of. We're at commercial.

August 3, 2008 at 5:08pm

ANNE PRESSLY wants Kevin Miller to know he can use her name whenever and however he wants :) He can even have it tattooed on him if he'd like!

July 31, 2008 at 7:05pm

ANNE PRESSLY is thinking that Kevin Miller should google image Justin Timberlake's cross tattoo before he commits at the tattoo parlor tomorrow.

July 28, 2008 at 10:26pm

ANNE PRESSLY is excited b/c the "W" trailer has been released! Here's a link to copy/paste. http://www.filmofilia.com/2008/07/28/oliver-stones-w-teaser-trailer/

July 28, 2008 at 11:48am

ANNE PRESSLY is both laughing at and thankful for our new trailer park portable air conditioners we have in the newsroom. Now I don't need Kevin's ONJ sweatband.

July 25, 2008 at 2:37pm

ANNE PRESSLY has a gigantic cardboard boat in the living room. Bet Kevin Miller can't guess why...

July 25, 2008 at 12:44am

ANNE PRESSLY just realized I misspelled a word in my last status update. Yes, I attended public school most of my life.

July 24, 2008 at 10:20am

ANNE PRESSLY has written some pointless news stories in my day, but the one I've been trying to cranck-out for nearly 2 hours is a doozie.

JULY 24, 2008 AT 7:57AM

ANNE PRESSLY is WAY silly. Even at 6:45 in the am.

JULY 24, 2008 AT 6:45AM

ANNE PRESSLY is wanting to know why Kevin Miller is not-so-secretly making fun of me!

JULY 23, 2008 AT 6:47PM

ANNE PRESSLY is back to work less than 12 hours after leaving. The air better work.

JULY 23, 2008 AT 6:24AM

ANNE PRESSLY is RIP Estelle Getty. Who didn't love Sophia?

JULY 22, 2008 AT 1:41PM

ANNE PRESSLY feels like I'm working for Kathie Lee Gifford. It's a freaking sweatshop in this newsroom!

JULY 22, 2008 AT 1:25PM

ANNE PRESSLY is at the vet. Sick puppies :(

JULY 21, 2008 AT 3:21PM

ANNE PRESSLY is tagging old-school photos. I really do have better things to do w/my time, but this is how I procrastinate!

JULY 19, 2008 AT 11:05AM

ANNE PRESSLY is feeling sorry for Miss USA and hoping she takes comfort in the fact that she still got an 8.050 in the evening gown competition after falling on her rear.

JULY 14, 2008 AT 12:11AM

ANNE PRESSLY is partying w/OS.

JULY 12, 2008 AT 11:19PM

ANNE PRESSLY is in Shreveport w/MDG for the "W" wrap party!!!

JULY 12, 2008 AT 9:40PM

ANNE PRESSLY wants to skip work today! No can do, though. Have a shoot @ 10:30. Why do I have to be such a planner?

JULY 11, 2008 AT 7:27AM

ANNE PRESSLY just got invited to the wrap party for "W" Saturday night. I must be a late add to the list. Anyone want to hang out w/Oliver Stone in Shreveport?

JULY 11, 2008 AT 12:27AM

ANNE PRESSLY is excited about LFT tonight...woo hoo!

JULY 10, 2008 AT 8:27AM

ANNE PRESSLY is heading home from a 12 hour day. In my car. Not on a scooter.

JULY 8, 2008 AT 6:41PM

ANNE PRESSLY is up early to follow the scooter couple and wondering how high gas would have to get before I invest in a cute Vespa.

JULY 8, 2008 AT 5:39AM

ANNE PRESSLY is doing a story on Arkansas' first chocolatier. Not a bad gig for a Monday!

JULY 7, 2008 AT 8:32AM

ANNE PRESSLY is thinking Mallory should go with the name Shimmy.

JUNE 28, 2008 AT 9:09AM

ANNE PRESSLY is on the way to Emerson for the Purple Hull Pea Festival Parade.

JUNE 28, 2008 AT 9:09AM
ANNE PRESSLY just killed a microphone with hairspray.

JUNE 27, 2008 AT 5:48AM
ANNE PRESSLY is sweating! No air in the newsroom or the studio...again. Beth, be glad you're off.

JUNE 27, 2008 AT 5:23AM
ANNE PRESSLY is up for Daybreak. So sleepy.

JUNE 26, 2008 AT 2:55AM
ANNE PRESSLY It's summertime! Jessica and Barry hosted a fun BBQ. I brought the bean dip. You'll see many artsy photos of it.

JUNE 25, 2008 AT 10:10PM
ANNE PRESSLY is in Pine Buff. Are y'all jealous?

JUNE 24, 2008 AT 1:07PM
ANNE PRESSLY stayed up WAY too late making layered dip for the BBQ tonight. Let's hope Paula Deen's recipe is worth the lack of sleep!

JUNE 24, 2008 AT 8:34AM
ANNE PRESSLY is thinking everyone will have a much better Monday if they go to YouTube and search "Crank Dat + Saved by the Bell." Trust me.

JUNE 23, 2008 AT 8:14AM
ANNE PRESSLY I know this album that I'm uploading at 1:45 in the morning is entiitled "Anthony Spits Game" and I realize that there's no Anthony in the pics. I get it. And so do the people whom I'm fixin to tag. Love y'all mean it

JUNE 22, 2008 AT 1:57AM
ANNE PRESSLY is still laughing about the marriage proposal I saw on the marquee at Church's chicken.

JUNE 21, 2008 AT 10:21AM
ANNE PRESSLY is headed home from The Circle Seven Ranch!

JUNE 20, 2008 AT 12:12AM
ANNE PRESSLY is doing Daybreak this morning and hoping Beth and Cam have a fun day together!

JUNE 19, 2008 AT 11:02PM
ANNE PRESSLY is pretty excited for Jeff and Tiffany!

JUNE 19, 2008 AT 10:45AM
ANNE PRESSLY is saying a prayer for Jamie-Lynn Spears's new baby girl.

JUNE 19, 2008 AT 10:19AM
ANNE PRESSLY is feeling awkward after looking at urbandictionary.com with her co-workers. Is that an employee handbook violation?

JUNE 18, 2008 AT 3:51PM
ANNE PRESSLY So there's this little karaoke bar called Classics at the HoJo on the Northside. No one knows about it. That's why we like it there

JUNE 17, 2008 AT 10:51PM
ANNE PRESSLY is thinking that Local Social Publication Bingo pretty much rocked.

JUNE 17, 2008 AT 8:57AM
ANNE PRESSLY is thrilled J-Mo is finally on the facebook.

June 16, 2008 at 7:54am
ANNE PRESSLY is watching Luke Russert on the Today Show

June 16, 2008 at 7:12am
ANNE PRESSLY had so much fun at Mary's baby shower! YAY!!!!

June 14, 2008 at 1:02pm
ANNE PRESSLY played with 10,000 angry bees this morning. All so you can watch them on Live at 5.

June 13, 2008 at 1:29pm
ANNE PRESSLY My job is never the same 2 days in a row. I got up at the crack of dawn to do a news story on on a honeybee hive at the Cathedral of St. Andrew. Heifer International removed the hive and took all 10,000 (not even kidding you) bees to the Heifer Ranch in Perryville. If you don't know about Heifer, you need to. It's only like the greatest non-profit ever. Heifer teaches the impoverished all over the world to become self-sufficient by raising cows, pigs, goats, or even honey bees. The only condition is that project recipients pass the gift on. These priceless photos of me in the most unattractive beekeeping outfit ever are my gifts I'm passing on to you.

June 13, 2008 at 1:16pm
ANNE PRESSLY is thankful the "celebrity" (term used loosely) flag football game was cancelled. I hate to sweat.

June 12, 2008 at 6:54pm
ANNE PRESSLY just finished a fun-filled edition of *Good Morning Arkansas*. Now on to my day job!

June 11, 2008 at 10:35am
ANNE PRESSLY is headed to Benton to do a story on bat infestation in an attic. You heard me. Bats.

June 10, 2008 at 10:19am
ANNE PRESSLY has somehow found herself watching Living Lohan. And she's thanking God her Mom is nothing like Dina.

June 8, 2008 at 11:47pm
ANNE PRESSLY can text again...YAY!

June 8, 2008 at 9:25pm
ANNE PRESSLY is OMG! I just realized my phone is not sending or receiving texts. Apparently, it hasn't been since Thursday. Call me if you need me, y'all!!!

June 7, 2008 at 11:38pm
ANNE PRESSLY is pretty much obsessed with the restaurant Za-Za.

June 6, 2008 at 12:25pm
ANNE PRESSLY just read Beth's status update and now dreads going to work.

June 6, 2008 at 7:51am
ANNE PRESSLY is thrilled!!!

June 5, 2008 at 6:33pm
ANNE PRESSLY thinks the view is always better atop new high heels.

June 5, 2008 at 8:50am
ANNE PRESSLY is back in AR from LA.

June 4, 2008 at 3:56pm
ANNE PRESSLY is RIP YSL.

JUNE 2, 2008 AT 5:45PM
ANNE PRESSLY is working the first day of a six-day week. Sounds worse than it really is.

JUNE 1, 2008 AT 11:30AM
ANNE PRESSLY is glad SATC did not disappoint...two Manolos up!

MAY 31, 2008 AT 2:11AM
ANNE PRESSLY is pumped to see her friends Carrie, Samantha, Charlotte and Miranda tonight!

MAY 30, 2008 AT 12:34PM
ANNE PRESSLY can't wait for SATC!

MAY 30, 2008 AT 12:21PM
ANNE PRESSLY is off today and tomorrow! YAY!

MAY 29, 2008 AT 9:38AM
ANNE PRESSLY is mourning the loss of her Prada to superglue. Any suggestions for some final attempts to get it out?

MAY 29, 2008 AT 3:55PM
ANNE PRESSLY is watching Noah Wylie have his makeup done.

MAY 27, 2008 AT 1:54PM
ANNE PRESSLY is hanging out w/OS. Not even kidding.

MAY 27, 2008 AT 11:56AM
ANNE PRESSLY is in Shreveport.

MAY 27, 2008 AT 7:47AM
ANNE PRESSLY is working...ugh...then headed to Shreveport tonight...YAY!!!

MAY 26, 2008 AT 12:48PM
ANNE PRESSLY Ok, so this pic has nothing to do with this album other than the fact I'm a nerd and felt the need to photograph the Villa Marre (the real name of the Designing Women house) between my 5 and 6 o'clock live shots when it snowed back in March. For those of y'all who are not Arkansans, all of the houses in the opening sequence of the show are actually located here in Little Rock, not Atlanta.

MAY 12, 2008 AT 9:47PM
ANNE PRESSLY just met The Donald!!!!! Photo to be uploaded soon.

MAY 8, 2008 AT 11:59AM
ANNE PRESSLY is headed to NWA to meet The Donald!

MAY 8, 2008 AT 7:10AM
ANNE PRESSLY is thanking God she's alive after flying in a crop duster.

APRIL 9, 2008 AT 2:31PM
ANNE PRESSLY met Maya Angelou today! Oh yeah, and Reuben Studdard, too...it was a big day...

MARCH 31, 2008 AT 6:52PM
ANNE PRESSLY hates live television sometimes. Like when she acts like an idiot. Like tonight at 6 o'clock.

MARCH 28, 2008 AT 6:53PM
ANNE PRESSLY is working on Saturday night. Yuck.

JANUARY 27, 2008 AT 1:40PM
ANNE PRESSLY is headed to South Carolina for the Primary!

Heather Crawford, Shilo Groover Korzen, Pamela Smith, Tomeca Sloan and Anne

January 15, 2008 at 11:29am

ANNE PRESSLY can't believe the tower fell.

January 11, 2008 at 3:39pm

ANNE PRESSLY is Cotton Bowl bound! One more early morning to endure first, though.

December 27, 2007 at 10:39pm

ANNE PRESSLY is working the Daybreak shift and needs a nap. 2:45 is just too early.

December 27, 2007 at 7:58am

ANNE PRESSLY The League Middle girls reunite for a evening of laughs at the Cafe and Then Some. Reunion in G-Vegas.

December 22, 2007 at 3:18pm

ANNE PRESSLY This might be my favorite night of the year. It's an annual event that raises money for Youth Home AND allows everyone from the governor to local tv folks to make fools of themselves at the same time. The Channel Seven girls' "Hey Mickey" performance was strong, but only good enough for 3rd place. Our own Jason Pederson took home the top honor for the second year in a row. 103.7 The Buzz Christmas Karaoke

December 18, 2007 at 5:13pm

ANNE PRESSLY Heather and Michael open their home to their TV family December 8.

December 14, 2007 at 9:53pm

ANNE PRESSLY is working. And it's Saturday night. You've got to be kidding me.

November 10, 2007 at 7:06pm

ANNE PRESSLY This pic is actually at a different Halloween party, but Melissa Dunbar Gates' costume is so classic that I had to include it in this album!

November 5, 2007 at 3:33pm

ANNE PRESSLY Susan G. Komen Race for the Cure. The Channel 7 girls were on stage at 4th and Main to cheer-on the 45 thousand walkers and runners. We had so much fun!

November 2, 2007 at 5:41pm

ANNE PRESSLY Send-off soiree for our beloved Tomeca before she moved to the ATL.

November 2, 2007 at 5:35pm

ANNE PRESSLY Staff picnic in June. The Travs were rained out, but our party was not!

November 2, 2007 at 5:34pm

ANNE PRESSLY Costume Party sponsored by 103.7 The Buzz.

November 2, 2007 at 4:19pm

PERMELICIOUS • Just for Fun - Totally Random
KATV Channel 7's Ned Perme. He's The Chief...meteorologist, that is. And he's fantastic.

October 31, 2007 at 5:33pm

ANNE PRESSLY Fundraiser for CARE for Animals. Clementine and Daisy modeled the latest doggy fashions. Their mommy, Anne, escorted them down the runway. Thanks to Stacey Stark for taking these!
October 29, 2007 at 4:02pm
Recent Activity

ANNE JOINED FACEBOOK

Anne and the Channel 7 crew on stage to cheer on the walkers and runners in the Susan G. Komen Race for the Cure, October 2007

Shilo Groover Korzen, Anne, Cassie Nicholson and Amanda Manatt

A TRUE FRIEND

Anne never met a stranger. She quickly befriended everyone she met. But beyond that, she took friendships very seriously. When she would ask, "How are you?" or "How's your family?" she sincerely wanted to know. If you were Anne's friend, she knew your spouse's name, your siblings' names, your children's names and even your friends' names. Not only did she remember their names, she got to know them. Once she had met you, there was nothing she wouldn't do for you. The way she could find time for others was uncanny.

"The last time I saw Anne was at my baby shower. Prior to my shower, she was the *only* person I let take a picture of me sideways. Who could say no to Anne? I remember she even put that picture on her Facebook page and tagged the baby, 'Natalee Noelle.' Now I look at that picture on her Facebook page with a heavy heart. We named our baby Natalee Anne in her honor. Anne died just three weeks before our daughter was born. She was so excited to meet Natalee and 'teach her how to shop,' to which my husband, Dale, would reply, 'Anne, I don't have the money for that!'

—*Cassie Nicholson, wife of Dale Nicholson III*

"I was looking for a teaching job and having a terrible time. I went up to the station just to visit everyone. When Anne heard how hard a time I was having, she instantly started working the phones, calling schools for me. She was waiting to go on an interview, and spent her down time working leads for me. I'll never, ever forget that. I had given up in a way, and she pretty much forced me to get out the phone book and continue my hunt. That was Anne. She wanted everyone to be happy and would go out of her way to make that possible."

—*Amanda Kelton, former KATV producer*

Randy Dixon, Dale Nicholson III, Cassie Nicholson, Shilo Groover Korzen, Heather Crawford, Anne and Kiristin Fisher

"She was in my grandson's wedding. We were at Eureka Springs and the wedding had been at Thorncrown Chapel and then the reception following — it was at the Crescent. You had to walk up six or seven flights of stairs to even get to the ballroom. Anne and the other female reporters from KATV were on the dance floor having such a grand time. She led the crowd that time, and I mean it turned into a celebration because of her. She was just the lead on that. She was just one of those people that could just turn the magic on."

—*Dale Nicholson, KATV president and general manager*

"Anne LOVED her dogs, Clementine and Daisy. She treated them as if they were her children. She also would give so much of her time to organizations that were raising funds or awareness for anything animal-related. The Humane Society of Pulaski County asked dog-owners at Channel 7 if we wanted our pets to be a part of a calendar of 'celebrity' dogs. So Anne, Jason Pederson and I brought our dogs, Clementine and Daisy, Alex, and Lucy, to a Little Rock park so Randy Dixon could take a picture of all of us. It was quite the task! But with a little effort (and a lot of patience!) we got a photo of almost all seven of us looking at the camera! It really was a lot of fun. And just one of the crazy things that may have taken a little time and effort but was so worth it!"

—*Christina Muñoz, KATV news anchor*

Anne, Jason Pederson and Christina Muñoz and their dogs

"The story I'd like to share with you about Anne involved baseball, my soon-to-be-born son, and her ability to think of others in the midst of one of the most exciting, chaotic times in her life. Anne let me know about a baseball sign that she had purchased and wanted to give it to us for his room. This all happened around the time she was in the middle of her trips to Shreveport, La., to film her scenes in 'W.'. Instead of me trying to tell it, I thought the best way for you to get the essence of why my family and I loved Anne would be best served through her own words. What follows is the conversation pulled from our Facebook walls and as you can see by the date and time stamps, it took us a few weeks to make this happen. Her awareness of what was going in our lives in the midst of her busy-ness is something that was always evident in her life.

Beckett Matthews and the sign Anne bought for him from Ray Winder

Anne Pressly: I know I'm the last person you'd expect to respond to your baseball memorabilia request, but as it turns out, I have one of the old signs from Ray Winder. It's signed by Bill Valentine. I got it when they had that yard sale a few months ago. I'm sentimental like that. Problem is, it doesn't so much match my decor. I'm thinking it will match Beckett's decor much better. If you want it, you're welcome to it! May 15, 2008 at 11:04pm

Jeff Matthews: I would LOVE to have that for Beckett's room! I will be able to tell him someday that his TV Aunt Anne gave it to him!! I really do appreciate it. May 16, 2008 at 6:24am

Anne Pressly: Great! It's propped-up by my desk at work. I can drop it by B98 before I go to Shreveport next week if you'd like. Or before then. Whatever works. May 16, 2008 at 8:42am

Jeff Matthews: You can do it whenever is best for you. We just really, really appreciate it! He won't be here until the middle of next month! May 16, 2008 at 4:47pm

Anne Pressly: Ok, I'm afraid Beckett is going to graduate from pre-school before he gets his Ray Winder sign, so I'm bringing it to you tomorrow. Would right after the show be cool? May 28, 2008 at 10:48pm

Jeff Matthews: That would be fine, and don't worry for a second about it. May 29, 2008 at 5:12pm

Jeff Matthews: Did you see the picture of Beckett's room that I posted??? Your sign is front and center! June 12, 2008 at 8:05am

Anne Pressly: Finally, something I'm good at! The nursery looks fabulous ... I can't wait to see more pictures of all the progress! June 12, 2008 at 8:09am

Beckett has turned one now and still falls asleep every night under that sign that his 'TV Aunt Anne' gave him. I can't wait for the day that he asks me about it and I can tell him about my sweet, generous friend who always put others first and always loved others with all her heart."

—*Jeff Matthews, B98 radio host*

Anne and Lisa Fischer

"When someone takes a special interest in your child you have a love for that. You know, as a mother with a teen-ager, I would love to have a daughter to grow up to be an Anne. She took such an interest in my 16-year-old daughter."

—*Lisa Fischer, B98 radio host*

*Pamela Smith and her son
Brandon with Anne*

"Anne was the type of person if she ever told you she was going to do something, I don't care what it took, she fulfilled her commitment. I happened to be helping with the NAMI walk, which is the National Alliance for the Mentally Ill. And it was a beautiful day and I think Anne had been out of town or something the night before and I thought that's the last thing she's going to want to do, but you see this little white convertible tooling around the corner at Burns Park and she showed up. And some of my other friends didn't show up, but Anne did; and I'm always going to appreciate her for that."
—*Pamela Smith, KATV weekend anchor*

"I would come into work mad about something or upset about something and I would almost get mad at her when I walked in because I *wanted* to be in a bad mood, but she wouldn't let me be in a bad mood because she would always have those jokes or a funny story."
—*Chris Scott, KATV producer*

"One reason Anne was such a special person was how she treated everyone. It didn't matter who they were or what they did, they were all made to feel special in some way. From the servers working at IHOP late at night to my young niece and nephew ... they were all made to feel special. Anne would wear little bracelets that my 4-year old nephew would send to her so he could see them when she was reporting. She also carried "Flat Stanley" around all day and took photos around the station and sent them all back to my niece with notes as part of her school project. Anne would go out of her way to do big things and little things for people just to make them feel special, even after working long shifts, and would always do it with a smile. I consider myself to be a very lucky person to have had the opportunity to be around Anne in many different settings around a lot of different people and see how she touched each and every person in a different unique way and made them all feel special.
— *Alan Faulkner, KATV assistant news director*

"My favorite memory of Anne will always be what she taught me about friendship. My husband and I lived 30 minutes north of Little Rock and Anne. I was a newlywed when Anne and I were at the height of enjoying time together. Sometimes seeing each other was tough because of distance and time. But Anne always had a way of making it easy. She consistently drove to my community to see my husband and me, even though most of Anne's friends and my friends/parties/gatherings were in her community. She invested in my life, in what was going on with me; embraced it and took it on as hers. She would even sit around a table with us and talk about rap music with my husband for hours ... while I never understood a word of it. Anne taught me friendship, real friendship. Friendship from God is all about the other person and not at all about ourselves. Love you Anne. Missing you, always ..."

—*Melissa Dunbar-Gates, KTHV reporter*

"Anne had an uncanny ability to remember people's names. She not only knew everyone's name in the building where she worked ... but she knew their spouses, their kids ... etc. Once we were talking about the Wal-Mart Supercenter near my house (It's relatively new). Anne says, "I love that Wal-Mart! I go out there and see Miss Betty ..." I didn't know who she was talking about at the time, but then after Anne's death I was walking into the Wal-Mart and there was the greeter who I usually saw at the entrance, handing out baskets. She would always say hi to me, but this time she said she just wanted me to know she was thinking of all of us at KATV. I stopped and said, "You must be Betty." And she was! Anne took the time to even learn and remember the name of the Wal-Mart greeter. I had passed by her so many times in a rush, but Anne had taken the time to stop and make her feel special. More lessons learned!"

—*Melinda Mayo, KATV meteorologist*

"I had my son, Ethan, about two weeks after we moved in. I had no idea that Anne lived behind me until there was a knock on my door. I opened it and their were two bright smiling faces. It was Anne and her mom with a basket of cookies and pastries. I was so excited because you don't eat when you have a new baby. I had them come in and Anne's mother introduced me to her. Anne said that she had watched Channel 7 forever and had wanted to be a Channel 7 reporter since she moved to Little Rock. Anne asked about where I went to college and we talked about the University of Missouri. I kind of decided right then and there that Anne was going to go to the University of Missouri. We talked through that and Anne and her mother became my friends, my little next-door-neighbor happy friends. You couldn't ask for a better present when you move in — I was meant to move into that house and we were meant to be in each other's life."

—*Joan Early, KATV reporter*

"She had this amazing ability to remember everybody's kid's names, their uncle's names, their cousin's names, and she would come back and ask you, you know 6 months from now, 'How's Noah?' Noah's my nephew. Or I have another little cousin that she would pay particular attention to when I would bring him up to the station and she would always ask how he was and I always thought that was a real gift that she connects with people on a real level as opposed to just two ships passing in the night. Because if you ask me to say some child's relative's name, I probably wouldn't remember. But she had a really, really amazing gift to be able to do it. And she seemed genuinely concerned when you told her a story about a relative because ... she could recite the circumstances verbatim if you ever asked her about it later, so that was a gift. When you connect with somebody that's a sign to me that you're a genuine person. You may say, 'Hey, how ya doing,' and the person could say, 'Oh, I'm sick,' and you say, 'Oh, that's great,' because you weren't even paying attention. But Anne would listen to you say you're not feeling well ... she might ask you a couple of days later, 'You feeling better, you know? Can I do anything for ya?' "

—*Pamela Smith, KATV weekend anchor*

"**She had this amazing ability to remember everybody's kid's names, their uncle's names, their cousin's names, and she would come back and ask you, you know 6 months from now, 'How's Noah?' Noah's my nephew.**"
—*Pamela Smith*

"If you were having a bad day, she would just say give me a hug and she knew you needed that hug. She didn't know my problems, but I needed those hugs. She had the boom. I liked her because she was genuine. She was a true angel. ... She was Annie May and I was Tyronnie May."

—*Tyrone McIntosh, KATV studio production*

Anne with Tyrone McIntosh, a member of KATV's studio production crew

"She was always giving, too. If you didn't have any money she would buy your lunch for you and then you could pay her back later and she always tried to give you directions on how to get to places. I told her I grew up here all my life. But you know some of her directions were good because she showed me some places that I didn't know."

—*Ray Hamilton, KATV photojournalist*

"I think I had been here about three weeks when my family came to town to visit me for the first time. Anne's mom happened to be in town that weekend, too. We were trying to figure out where to go to dinner and she was like, 'Well, we're going to Pizza Cafe, why don't you come?' Inviting this person she barely knew and the entire family that she barely knew to have dinner with her and her mom ... that sense of welcoming and wanting to make everyone feel like they fit in was so special. It's something to look back on and it's easy to appreciate, but at the time I didn't realize how much of an impact that made on me and my whole family. I mean my whole family was like 'This place is great' and 'Wow, Anne's just like her mom!' And it really made everyone feel so special ... that was a unique skill that she possessed, to make everyone feel special."

—*Shilo Groover Korzen, KATV producer*

"The last movie I saw with Anne was 'The House Bunny' at the Riverdale theater. She knew I got cold at movies — so she walked in with a huge stack of blankets into the theater! I laughed and so did the other people inside! They told her they had never seen anyone bring blankets into a movie before. She of course loved that, that she was the first! Watching movies with Anne was so much fun — she would always laugh out loud and clap her hands in the air through the entire movie. She made it better for everyone in the theater!"

—*Mallory Hardin, KARK reporter*

"Anne owned every room she walked into. Her energy and smile and good nature was palpable. She was silly and wasn't afraid to make fun of herself. She loved to make others laugh. She would say you can never be too blonde or too thin ... and then laugh hysterically ... and indeed she got blonder as I knew her. But the thing about Anne is that she remembered the little things and really listened to you. And if she could do something to make your day better she would do it. I remember when I moved into my first house on Midland Street in the Hillcrest section of Little Rock she was the first one to buy me a housewarming present. She had hand-painted a plate with an exact replica of my little house on Midland and had written the quote "A home is a place that shelters the body and feeds the soul." It was such a beautiful and thoughtful thing to do. That was Anne, always doing little things like that. She was a very unique and special person and I am infinitely grateful that I had the privilege of knowing her. I can feel her life and love all around us."

—*Kate Sullivan, former KATV news anchor*

LIVE

Crazy 'bout Cotton **Dallas, TX**
Hyatt Regency

Anne covering the 2008 Cotton Bowl with Abbey and Ashton Inman

"I still remember the 2008 Cotton Bowl. We were down there for the special, and I remember she put my daughters on TV. She was really special for my twins, her and Jessica Dean both, because they would always put makeup on them and were always good to give them a lot of attention. My kids would always like to come to the newsroom because they knew they would be the center of attention. And they would get a lot of attention from Anne. And they asked about her a lot to. She was good with my kids."

—Scott Inman, KATV news anchor

"A nne would go out of her way to talk to and befriend people for no other reason than that she was a friendly and caring person. After her death, Arthur, the janitor, told me that he had seen Anne at a shopping center, and she had hollered across the parking lot for him to come over and talk to her so she could ask what he was doing that day. Everybody chit chats with co-workers because they are together at work, but Anne would spend time away from work talking to people just to be friendly. Anne had a way of making people feel special because of the special way she treated them. I have trouble keeping in touch with my family and relatives, much less a lot of friends. I don't know how Anne found the time to be a special friend to so many people, and I wonder when she ever found time to sleep?"

—Charles Young, KATV engineer

"A nne was so friendly and easy to talk to. She really made me feel a part of the group from the word go. She always had a way of making you feel like she *really* cared about what was going on in your life."

—Cassie Nicholson, wife of Dale Nicholson III

"S he had a spirit about her that was just unique among the people that have been through this station, and a lot of great personalities have been through here. But you couldn't walk through the newsroom without Anne acknowledging you. And engineers would come to me who have been here 20, 30 years and don't have a lot of connection with on-air people, and would always say, 'Anne asked me how I'm doing, how my family is.' She was that genuine. She was that sincere. She wanted everyone to be as happy as she was."

—Dale Nicholson, KATV president and general manager

"Anne was tall. Considerably taller than me. I was in my late 40s, and not having any children, it became a running gag between us that she was the 'tall daughter I never had.' She would occasionally call me 'Daddy Bill.' I would begin e-mails to her with 'What's up daugh?' I'm very grateful for that gag. Because it was more than a gag. I suspect she was indeed the closest thing to a daughter I will ever have. What a blessing."

—*Bill Dailey, former KATV satellite truck operator*

"All these people would say, oh she came and visited me in the hospital, oh she used to go walking with me and my dog and I thought, 'When did this girl have time to do all this?' It wasn't really surface level, she really got to know people and people were very important to her, relationships were very, very important to her. There are very few people who can walk into a room and almost connect to everybody in that room and make them feel, when she was talking to you, you're the only person. And she was going to move her hands and she was going to yell at you and she was going to sing a song and she might kind of wiggle around a little bit and that's what made it so fun and people wanted to be next to her. When you went to a party or dinner, whatever table she was sitting at, that was the table to be at because that was the fun table. That was the loud and slightly inappropriate table and that's where you wanted to be."

—*Jessica Dean, KATV reporter*

"Anne treated everyone with the same respect, from the president of the company to the people cleaning the building. She spent time with just about everybody and engaged them in conversation and made them feel like she was interested. And I'm pretty sure she *was* interested. I am going to miss that girl. I love you, Anne."

—*Stewart McLendon, KATV chief editor*

"I can remember the first time my wife met her was the weekend that everyone went to see 'W.' So we saw her at the movie theatre and she just ran up to my wife and said, 'You must be Christie,' and gave her a big hug and my wife was just kind of like, 'Who's this crazy girl?' I was like "That's Anne. That's who she is, she's that outgoing and everything.' "

—*Finley Turner, KATV weekend assignment editor*

"You have different friends that have different attributes and hers was: She's your fun friend. Your friend you want to go to, to cheer you up, to make you laugh, to make you smile; and she always, always had a smile on her face."

—*Heather Crawford, KATV anchor/reporter*

"I had broken up with a boy, a guy that I had been seeing ... and I was really upset about it. This was when Anne was working in Jackson, Miss., and she was home that weekend. We were talking on the phone and I said I couldn't believe what was happening ... I didn't know how this was going to play out. And she said, 'I'm on my way.' She came over and got me and we drove back over to Memphis to her apartment and then eventually on down to Jackson. We then spent the day and subsequent evening and it was just, we're getting you out of Little Rock. You need to be out of Little Rock; you don't have to think about him' ... and we did!"

—*Michelle Rupp, KATV reporter*

"Anne treated everyone with the same respect, from the president of the company to the people cleaning the building ... I am going to miss that girl..."
—*Stewart McLendon*

Leslie and Rebecca Dixon in coordinating outfits that Anne selected especially for them

"My daughters loved Miss Anne. After my divorce, I had a hard time with a couple of young girls and Anne stepped in to help. She had a great sense of style and whenever I needed clothes for the girls I looked to Anne. I would give her a budget and she would get online and hit dozens of websites and pick out great outfits. She said it was like dressing up real live dolls. Speaking of dolls, we were in Dallas covering the Cotton Bowl. Before we left, she *had* to stop at the Galleria to shop. There was a place there called American Girl, a doll store. OK, a really *big,* kind of upscale doll store. I had never heard of it. Before we left for Little Rock, she had picked out dolls that looked like each of my daughters and talked me into getting matching outfits for them."

—*Randy Dixon, KATV news director*

"She always had my best interests … I mean there were times I just didn't want to be bold and stand up for myself and she always put that in me, that you have to or else, you know, no one else will. So she definitely gave me the fight and I admire her and learned so much from her. I wouldn't trade a minute for the world."

—*Courtney Dixon, KATV production assistant*

"She had a special connection with children. She seemed to be drawn to them and them to her. Anytime we had kids in the newsroom to do interviews, they would just flock to her and she would get down on their level and engage them and talk one on one with them. She did that with Cameron, too. She invited us over and she walked him around in her neighborhood in the Heights. They would pet cats in the neighborhood and walk around for about an hour and they loved it, both of them loved it. To this day when people come to the studio and they are on this show, the first thing they want to know about is Anne. I was at this reading event a couple of weeks ago at the Governor's Mansion and the kids were going crazy and there was this one kid sitting in the middle and he looked up at me and goes, 'Did you know Anne Pressly and were you friends with Anne Pressly?' I said, 'Yes' and he looked down and he looked back up and he had tears in his eyes. This kid was in the second grade there and he said, 'I'm so sorry,' and it was just a true testament to how she was living her life — that she was touching people that she hadn't even met before."

—*Beth Hunt, KATV morning anchor*

"I had a huge box of birthday cards and Valentine's Day cards and I was trying to go through them and I found one that I had forgotten. She had written me on my first birthday here and that would have been August. She was 26 and would have her birthday 4 days after me. We were very close in our birthdays and I had given her some Diet Coke with a big bow on it for her birthday or something. And it said: 'Dear Jessica, Thank you so much for the Diet Coke. It's already been put to great use. I'm so happy you've come home to Channel 7. I couldn't have picked a better place for you, and I'm so happy that you're here and that you're home.' And she made this workplace feel like a home, and it already has that feeling. I think it's a really special place to work but beyond that I think she made it even more so because she took a special interest in everybody and I think that was something."

—*Jessica Dean, KATV reporter*

A visualization by Aaron Malyk, KATV Senior Web Producer, of the most commonly used words in sentiments submitted to the Anne Pressly: Your Thoughts and Prayers page.

In the hazy hours and days that followed Anne's attack and eventual passing, the Station's website was overwhelmed with condolences. Such immense tragedy - an unusually bright, pure and hopeful life so senselessly ended - drew from the hearts of scattered, uncommon strangers a common sympathy. Each word of thousands of messages to Anne, her family and friends had to be read before publishing. Genuine expressions of sadness and comfort, all unique, yet so similar each to the other; so numerous that Anne's loved ones could never be expected to read each one. For that reason, it seemed appropriate to capture, visually, the essence of the messages. The result can be seen above - thousands of voices in one picture. The more frequently a word was used, the larger it is represented. Though the positioning of the words was at random, there would almost appear to be some purpose behind the resultant harmony.

12/15/04

"For, after all, the important thing for us as Christians is not what we eat or drink but stirring up goodness and peace and joy

12/20/04

"In all thy ways acknowledge Him, and He shall direct their paths."

Proverbs 3:6

12/21/04

"Then make me truly happy by loving each other, working together with one heart and mind and purpose."

Philippians 2:2

12/29/04

"You search the scriptures, for you believe they will give you eternal life. And the Scriptures point to me! Yet you won't come to see me so that I can give you this life eternal."

John 5:39-40

from the Holy Spirit."
Romans 14:17

12/23/04

"I will give you one heart and a new spirit; I will take you from your hearts of stone and give you tender hearts of love for God."

Ezekiel 11:19

ANNE'S FAITH

Anne was loud about everything except her faith. She was deeply spiritual but never pushed her beliefs on others. Anne was raised in the church and had a personal relationship with God and Jesus Christ. She wouldn't be the first to bring it up but if given the opportunity she would share unabashedly. She took part in bible studies and was continuously in search of a stronger faith.

"Everyday she would go to this website that had scriptures of the day. I don't know what website it was because there are many different websites that do it. It just gives you a scripture a day for you to just keep in mind as you go throughout the day. That's really the only time of day I noticed that she was quiet writing it down on a post-it note and sticking it on her computer. One day I said, 'Do you do that everyday?' and she said yes. She said, 'You just got to, you gotta do it sometimes, you gotta do it. It just gets you through the day.' And the only one I remember was Hebrews 12. I don't know if she was having a bad day or what, but I looked it up and it said, 'Make every effort to live in peace with all men and to be holy, without holiness no one will see the Lord.' So that's the only scripture that I remember. I look back at it and I was like wow so I thought that was pretty neat."

—*Beth Hunt, KATV morning anchor*

"It became obvious I wasn't cut out for news, so I began career hunting. Anne was a constant source of advice and inspirational words when I felt like I just couldn't handle it anymore. I still have some scriptures Anne wrote out and taped to my computer. She was ALWAYS taking care of other people. If you needed advice about shoes or an outfit ... no question, ask Anne. Need to know the scoop on practically anything? She usually knew that, too. And if she didn't, she would soon find out for you."

—*Amanda Kelton, former KATV producer*

"**A**nne always had the perfect thing to say to make someone feel better. Especially when it came to problems with relationships! She told me to never settle, and to live by these words: 'Find a man who loves the Lord and makes you laugh!' I will never forget those wise words!"

—*Mallory Hardin, KARK reporter*

"**Y**ou know I tell God if I don't see any more angels I know I crossed paths with one in my lifetime, that I did."

—*Tyrone McIntosh, KATV studio production*

"**O**ne morning before *Daybreak* we were getting ready in the dressing room. Anne normally came in bouncing ... usually singing a song or something. It would instantly cheer me up. On this day, though, she was more serious ... so I knew something was wrong. I asked her if she was OK, and she told me a story about a friend from her Bible study. The friend, a 20-something girl, had apparently just lost her mother. The mother, as Anne told me, was keeping the girl's new baby for a few hours. The girl had returned home to find her mother on the floor dead from an apparent aneurism. The mother had just collapsed, and the baby was lying on the floor beside her crying. The baby was fine, fortunately, but Anne felt so sad that her friend had to go through such a traumatic experience in losing her mother. Anne was really torn up about it and asked me to pray for the family. Anne cared so deeply about others. ... and the fact that this friend and her family were on Anne's mind first thing in the morning is evidence of that. Even more ... the fact that Anne would tell others about it and ask them to say a prayer for them. It just shows that she was like an angel on Earth ... always thinking of others and lifting them up."

—*Beth Hunt, KATV morning anchor*

"Everything has its time (Ecclesiastes 3) ... Who would have known **WE** were on the clock?"
—*Tomeca Sloan, former KATV producer*

"I liked the spirit in her. That's not a man-made spirit, that's a gift. If we look at Anne, we see the joy that Anne had. I'm not trying to preach to you here, but the joy that Anne had, other prophets and people of the Good Book had that joy. I look at Anne as the young lady that brought joy not only to this newsroom but in Magnolia, Camden and everywhere we went. If you were sad, you weren't going to be sad long around Anne because there was something about her that was going to make you laugh. Even when you wanted to be mad, you couldn't be mad around Anne. She was also very religious. I told Anne I was going to be ordained as a deacon and she said, 'I'm coming.' I'm Baptist. Anne was of a different denomination, but when you are of God it doesn't matter what you call yourself. I looked over and saw Anne was up clapping and dancing. The people at my church still talk about the Anne Pressly they saw having a good time. You look back and say, 'What's that girl from Channel 7 doing here,' but they saw the joy in her. Before she died we had a conversation about heaven and hell and we were laughing and talking. I said you sure better hope I ain't at the gate. I'm gonna send you to the left and call security to come and get you. I'm gonna say security come get her, take her on down there. And she said, 'No, Marcus, I'm going to heaven.' I do believe that Anne can get there herself, and if we practice what she did we can get there, too. You know this life is temporary. But, like I say, if a person lives a short a time and can do the things she did, bring joy to the homeless and everybody else, that one moment is good enough."
—*Marcus McDonald, KATV photojournalist*

"I liked the spirit in her. That's not a man-made spirit, that's a gift. If we look at Anne, we see the joy that Anne had..."
—*Marcus McDonald*

"Jason Pederson talked about Anne reading *The Shack* by William Young. My oldest daughter, Tonya had bought and read that book, and she loaned it to me. Aside from the violent death portrayed in the story, I am not surprised that Anne was entertained and curious about the wacky and fanciful way that "God" was portrayed in the book. Maybe I cannot know the full extent of what life, death, and God is all about, but I know at least that Anne Pressly's short life had a positive impact on a lot of people including me. I miss you, Anne."

—*Charles Young, KATV engineer*

Anne with Bill Dailey's dog Nettie

"As I got to know Anne better, I really started to learn about her strong faith. She was raised by strong Christian parents ... and it showed. And I remember when things got a little rough in the newsroom (which happened often), she would announce in her signature loud voice, 'I need a little Jesus!' That usually meant she would look up a Bible verse or go to a Bible study or conference the next day. Whatever it took to get her mind out of negativity and back to where it needed to be. We usually laughed when she said it but I later realized that she meant it."

—*Christina Muñoz, KATV news anchor*

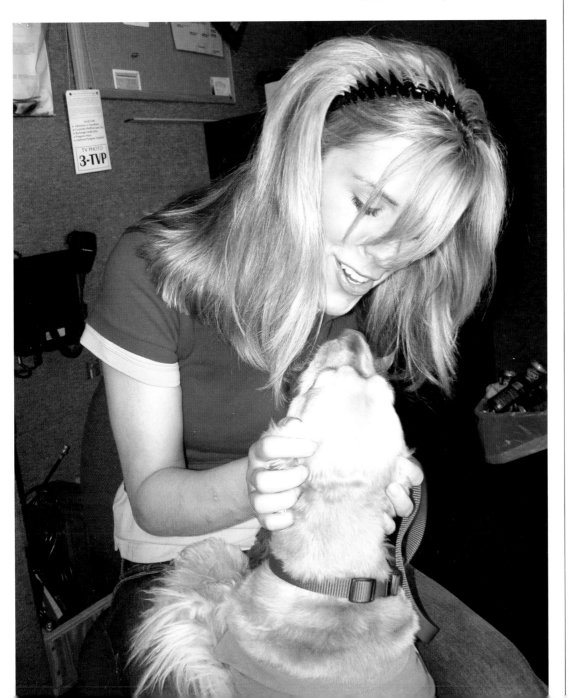

Anne with one of beloved cocker spaniels

Dale Nicholson sharing the limelight with Anne in the KATV studio

THE REAL ANNE

Television personalities are multi-faceted. They can be serious news reporters one day and be riding a Ferris wheel at the state fair the next. Anne was exceptionally good at versatility.

And while viewers got to know her through her reports, her friends and colleagues saw so much more. The "off-camera" Anne, the real Anne, was bigger than life.

"I remember they were doing some kind of story for a magazine and they wanted a picture of me on the anchor desk downstairs. I had my best suit on that morning and I had put the makeup on a little bit to cover up these old lines. Anne was over in the corner on what we call the CNN desk for awhile and she saw what was going on. The photographer was shooting and she just came over, sat down on the anchor desk sprawled out. She put it on her Facebook page and that afternoon my son, who is the GM in Phoenix, e-mailed me saying, 'Who's this beautiful lady you're with on the anchor desk?' "

—*Dale Nicholson, KATV president and general manager*

"I think we've gotta talk about her dancing, because she did it everywhere. It didn't matter if she was in her own house or singing karaoke, she would spontaneously bust into dancing. One time she said. 'I'm going to dance like no one was in the room.' "

—*Beth Hunt, KATV morning anchor*

"**S**he just made everybody feel important and I think that it really came through sometimes. Like I said, the very thing that could annoy you about Anne is what made her endearing. She made time for everybody. She'd stop ... you can't go to the mall or to a restaurant with her without her stopping to talk to people she didn't even know. She really embraced the relationships that come with being on TV. She embraced it and so I think that that's part of her legacy for sure."

—*Amanda Manatt, KATV reporter*

"**U**p dancing in the newsroom, singing, clapping, once you were in the newsroom you just couldn't miss Anne — or *anywhere* — you just couldn't miss Anne. She had such a presence, always happy. You rarely saw here in a bad mood, and she always came back from the field with the best stories."

—*Angela Rachels, KATV assignment editor*

"**S**he was one beautiful person. Beautiful personality. Whenever she saw you, she was going to make sure that she said 'Hi' to you. One Saturday, I was at a place and she was covering a story and I tried to pretend like I didn't see her, and she said, "Oh no, you see me!" So I pulled over so we could talk. She's a sweet person. I wish I could bring her back. Wonderful, beautiful person."

—*Arthur Johnson, KATV maintenance crew*

"**S**he was so pleasant, so outgoing, so looking forward to tomorrow. Some people get up and dread tomorrow; Anne looked forward to it, and she could make such a difference. On the morning show she'd go to Magnolia or places like that way South of our viewing area and they'd turn out by the thousands or hundreds at least to see her! I mean, they wanted to be around a person with such a great spirit as Anne had."

—*Dale Nicholson, KATV president and general manager*

"**A**lan Faulkner would threaten to separate us if we didn't use our inside voices, so that was great fun."
—*Jessica Dean, KATV reporter*

"**P**eople in television often let their careers in the spotlight define who they are. The notoriety, the compliments, the success can consume a person and become their driving force in life. For Anne, her passion was to just be real. She wanted real friendships, real love, real happiness. She wanted to make a difference in people's lives ... and did she ever. I'll never forget that beaming smile and her saying to me, "What up J Hizzy?" Her glowing light will never be extinguished."

—*Jason Harper, former KATV morning host*

"I was working Saturday *Daybreak* Halloween of 2007. I think Anne was filling in for Pederson. Each Halloween the Saturday Daybreak Crew really gets into the costumes. I didn't realize until that morning that she had gotten permission to change into a costume after the last news block. Then, I see Anne appear in an evening gown, sash, crown and of course extremely high heels and we start playing a video clip from some pageant. She had dressed up as "Miss South Carolina Teen USA 2007." She didn't just stand there to look like her. She did the cooking segment at the end of the show in character throwing in random "US Americans" and "like such as" up to the end of the show."
— *Diana Harbour, KATV producer*

"She always knew how to make people laugh, how to make people smile. and it was just those impressions [that would] crack me up all the time. And other stories, when she would work the weekend or have to do *Daybreak* on the weekend, I would come in from a long night or something and she would make fun of me for being out all night doing crazy stuff and I would tell her stories about what was going on. ... I was always happy to have her smile because it was just a great thing to see."
— *Finley Turner, KATV weekend assignment editor*

"She was always dancing ... always the life of the party."
— *Heather Crawford, KATV anchor/reporter*

Anne dressed up for Halloween as Miss South Carolina Teen USA 2007

"My favorite memory of Anne has to be the day I got married. After the wedding we all went out dancing. Anne was drinking the regular ... two large Diet Cokes. She told us of this dance she knew called the "alligator." I had never heard of it and before I could ask her to show me Anne got down on the dance floor on her back and kicked her arms and legs like an alligator stuck on its back. It was completely random and quite hilarious, but that was just Anne. Funny, loud, silly, beautiful Anne."
— *Jamie Deason, former KATV producer*

"I remember one time my wife came to pick me up, because one of our cars has the tendency to not work that often, and one night in particular we were trying to leave somewhere. I forget where we were going but we were trying to get somewhere pretty quick after the show and ended up staying in the sports office for an hour and a half talking to Anne. My wife and her are just jabbering back and forth ... she had the tendency to slow you down if you were in a hurry because she'd get you into some conversation."
— *Dale Nicholson III, KATV weekend sports anchor*

"She sang. One time I told her, I said, 'Anne, you're a really good reporter,' and she thought I was really giving her a compliment, which I was because she is a really good reporter, 'but the singing, not so much, you might not wanna do that.' She was sweet."
— *Katrina Dupins, KATV producer*

Anne loved to dance

BEN KRAIN

"On my first day of work at KATV, our news director, Randy Dixon, told me to tag along with Anne on an assignment. As we waited for the photographer, Anne kept popping Hot Tamales in between sips of Diet Coke all while giving me the dish on the Circle 7 Ranch. She instantly made me feel like I had found a friend. On the drive to the shoot, Anne sat shotgun while photographer, Rich Newman, manned the wheel. We were just eating Hot Tamales and listening to some Top 40 tunes, when all of a sudden Anne did something I would have never dreamed this beautiful Southern Belle would do. Project Pat was playing and Anne just started belting the lyrics, "Good googly moogly, that thang is juicy." Over and over. It didn't take much to get Rich to join in. "Good googly moogly, that thang is juicy." It was a ridiculous song and they were quite a sight at 10 a.m. on a Monday morning. I was just sitting in the backseat half in awe, half wondering 'where am I?' But that was when I knew I was going to love this station."

—*Kristin Fisher, former KATV reporter*

"I know it's been said a million times how wonderful a person she is and her personality and I don't think anyone could ever match that. She's just a ... she's just a nut case first and foremost. She's off her mind crazy and just taller, bigger than life as a personality, but ... walked around with confidence also."

—*Mark Rose, KATV general sales manager*

"When you Google the phrase "full of life," a picture of Anne Pressley should appear. To say that she was that would be a serious understatement. A life so young, a heart so warm, a smile so bright that it was absolutely infectious ... that was Anne."

—*Jason Harper, former KATV morning host*

"To me, it was like, when you hung out with Anne all of a sudden it was like you got to hang out with the homecoming queen. I mean that's what she was. Everybody loved her. She was this ray of light and when you were with her you know you got some of that coolness too, or some of that light shined on you, too ..."

—*Melinda Mayo, KATV meteorologist*

"The time when she reworked the lyrics of "Fergalicious" to Permalicious — a tribute to Ned Perme. "Permalicious, definition make the weather Loco.""

—*Jessica Morkert, former KATV reporter*

"Permalicious was, well I've missed the curb on a lot of stuff on the Internet and things like that, but that was a song by Fergie, I think. I forgot the name of the real song — Fergalicious, that's right. She created Permalicious and she had, I think, Facebook and she actually put me into her Facebook [page] or whatever until my daughter saw it and got me out of there, and said you're getting too old for that. ... Anne kind of made the words up and I don't remember what they were but it was a song about me."

—*Ned Perme, KATV chief meteorologist*

Anne with Ned Perme

"We didn't have to say a lot to each other. That was the funny thing about Anne and myself. You know, I was old enough to be her dad, but we just had kind of a real close relationship and I think to be honest with you it was formed around humor, sort of sarcastic, a little biting, but a nice sense of humor. And we both kind of had that same sort of sense of humor. But we would just make fun of things. I think that's the one thing I remember, is that she just fit right into where I was going and I fit right in to where she was going as far as kind of making fun or just observing funny, stupid things in life. We would just go off on the Watson commercials, remember the pool and spa people? I would be the old man and she would be the young daughter in those commercials and we would just have a great time just making it up, you know like spa sales and bar stools 20 percent off. And we would just do those commercials in the newsroom and just make fun of so many things."

—*Ned Perme, KATV chief meteorologist*

"How sweet she was. And every time I see her she was the same person. Every time. She was just like my baby. She was just like my baby. If she had seen me no matter where she was, even if it wasn't here, she'd scream and holler "Miss Bettie!" You know, scream real loud. Lord, that's Anne. But I loved her to death. I really do. And I miss her really bad. I really do. And I always talked to her like I was her mother. Just talked to her."

—*Bettie Johnson, aka "Miss Bettie," KATV maintenance crew*

"I loved making Anne laugh so hard that no sound would come out. It wasn't that hard to do, but if she was begging me to stop or she couldn't hardly breathe and no sound was coming out, I got a lot of enjoyment out of that. It was really fun to get her to that place and like I said, it wasn't that hard to do."

—*Jason Pederson, KATV consumer reporter*

"I also remember how truly funny and quick Anne was. The last time I saw her was the Saturday before she was attacked. She came to one of my wedding showers and we talked about how exciting it was that 'W' came out and how shocked she was that she made the cut into the movie. Of course, none of us were surprised because she's amazing! I remember we actually turned on SNL because Tina Fey and Sarah Palin were going to be on together. When it was over Anne started doing a Sarah Palin impression and we were all in stitches. She always captivated a room."

—*Sandra Kirk, KLRT reporter*

"I think one of my favorite memories was, we were having a couple of people over to Dave's condo and we had a bunch of Air Force guys there and Anne and maybe Kristen, just a couple of my friends there, and Anne started singing, which is not surprising at all; she would sing everywhere. But Anne started singing and acting out that scene from Dirty Dancing, the lover boy scene. She's crawling across the floor acting it out and now I don't even remember why — she was trying to make a point of some kind — and everyone in the room just stopped and looked at her and went, like, what are you up to? She didn't care that everybody was looking at her ... she was making a point to me and Kristen and didn't care what anybody else had to say, because she went ahead and went with it. But then everybody got involved ... she included everyone else. Whatever the joke was that she was telling us at the time was just so heartwarming. And her ability to remember songs and change the words to them was one of my favorite things about her."

—*Shilo Groover Korzen, KATV producer*

"Anne was this incredible ball of energy who would explode into a room and be the center of attention. It's not like she demanded, she commanded. And without effort. It was just kind of her nature."

—*Randy Dixon, KATV news director*

"What I remember most is her smile and her laughter. She was just open-minded and open-hearted. She made you feel good no matter what. She was the first one that opened up and started talking when I first started. Just a good-hearted person."

—*Stanley Austin, KATV maintenance crew*

"Anne made reporter and started working on the evenings, same shift as me. This was good for me; I got to know her. We talked about our families and our upbringings. We laughed about the shows we watched on TV ... I loved her sense of humor and I think she liked mine ... at least she laughed at my jokes and observations on life. Her laugh, which I once thought was annoyingly loud, was a bright spot in my day. I figured the more I made her laugh, her laugh got louder. If I was really funny, she would snort with a high pitch inhale. That's when you knew she was tickled. I love that she was loud in announcing her presence. It created a call-and-response in the newsroom as everyone was glad to see her. I miss her wonderful laugh. It was boisterous and clearly indicative of her spirit. I love her self-deprecation. She was beautiful and smart, but had the same insecurities as everyone else. She used humor to deflect comments. This trait endeared her to others."

—*Stewart McLendon, KATV chief editor*

"I always look from the sports term, and I looked at her and said man, that's an athlete. Truth be told, Anne did not have an athletic bone in her body, but she had a great spirit."

—*Steve Sullivan, KATV sports director*

"From assisting me with booking 25 guests a week for *Good Morning Arkansas* to training to take over the show ... that's when our time together began to tell its story. Over time Anne traded her name in for "White Barbie" ... and me, well I was no longer Tomeca. Instead, I was "Black Barbie." Together we were a team of characters we'd made up in our own minds; two "Barbies" up for anything that came with a giggle."

—*Tomeca Sloan, KATV producer*

"I put her on the Paul Eells team. Can there be a higher honor? People like Anne and Paul. Unfortunately bad things happen to good people and she was one of the best. Still miss her to this day."

—*Tommy Smith, 103.7 The Buzz radio host*

"Every day was something new. If it was the latest hip hop dance, like the Soulja Boy, we were all trying to learn it. She would say come on, and she taught me how to do the Soulja Boy."

—*Tyrone McIntosh, KATV studio production*

"Anne was this incredible ball of energy who would explode into a room and be the center of attention..."
—*Randy Dixon*

Anne's desk

A LIFE THAT LIVES ON

Anne is gone but certainly not forgotten. Her life lives on in all of us who knew her. And we are all better for being a part of her life. There are so many ways Anne continues to touch others.

Not the least of which was the gift of life given through her donated organs. And even to many who did not have the opportunity to know her, Anne's story has changed lives.

"My only regret is that she was at the radio station a couple of days before she was attacked and I was trying to get ready for the show while I was talking to her in my office. I wish now that I would have focused 100 percent of my attention on her and our conversation. That has helped me to slow down and really give every encounter with friends and loved ones the attention it deserves because as we learned the hard way, you never know when or if you may see that person again."

—*Justin Acri, former KATV sports anchor*

"Annie May we miss you so much. It's way too quiet here without you. I see something every day that reminds me of you, and for that I am grateful — anything pink or sparkly, Diet Coke cans ... things that are so random, yet bring back so many fun memories. Thank you for your friendship. Love you, Akel."

—*Amanda Kelton, former KATV producer*

"I'm a few years older than her and I always thought of her as a little sister but then I got to thinking about it ... that advice that she would give ... she is so much wiser than her 26 years. And it was just neat for me to get to know her in those private moments. I think it's interesting how leading up to her death it seems like she was placed in so many people's lives in a different way. Like if she hadn't been put on that morning show we wouldn't have gotten as close as we had. I just think that's interesting that she just seemed to be ... it was almost like God was putting her in people's lives, sort of preparing for, for that."

—*Beth Hunt, KATV morning anchor*

"Really, I have learned a lot from Anne. In life, she taught me to care for others and be willing to listen to everyone. In death, she has taught me to hold on to the things that last and let go of the rest. Friends come and go, but rarely do you meet one as true as Anne."

—*Cassie Nicholson, wife of Dale Nicholson III*

"I want to add that I am so thankful that I had the chance to get to spend more time with Anne the last few months she was here. This will be cheesy, but it's the truth: Her faith, open heart and amazing, fun personality will have a lasting impact on my life."

—*Diana Harbour, KATV producer*

"She packed so much in to every single day. There's not one day that she sat around and didn't do anything. She was always around people ... always going, going, going, going. And looking back, her life makes complete sense. She only had a short time on Earth but packed so much into it. For being here for 26 years she did so much and went to so many places and met so many people and really she touched so many lives in such a positive way."

—*Heather Crawford, KATV anchor/reporter*

"For my 24th birthday, Anne gave me a card of two old ladies floating in inner tubes in a pool. She wrote, "This is us by the pool in about 50 years." I would give anything to have all those years to make memories with her, but the two years of memories that I do have are enough to last a lifetime. Anne taught me to live harder, to love fuller, and to make every single moment count. I miss you so much. Love you, mean it."

—*Kristin Fisher, former KATV reporter*

"I think she let us all live life in such a way that we'll never forget it. We'll — I will never be the same because of the things I learned and the wisdom I gleaned from a young girl who really had a lot of wisdom, who really had her head on straight. She's really unique. I mean I don't think I've ever known anyone like her and I don't think I ever will."

—*Lisa Fischer, B98 radio host*

"When we had our baby girl we decided, after everything that happened, to name our daughter after Anne. And I remember having a hard time with the idea that Anne wasn't here to meet her. Anne always talked about how much she wanted to take her shopping. Cassie just opened a Facebook account recently and came across a picture that she had been tagged in by Anne and Anne had tagged "the baby to be," you know, when Cassie was pregnant with Natalie Noel, the original name that we picked out for her. That was two weekends ago when we saw that, it was kind of that epiphany that she didn't even know we changed the name. ... She knows now, though."

—*Dale Nicholson III, KATV weekend sports anchor*

"She packed so much in to every single day. There's not one day that she sat around and didn't do anything. She was always around people ... always going, going, going, going..."
—*Heather Crawford*

"I knew the real Anne, I knew the little girl all the way to Channel 7, because she told me. So I knew the real Anne and I knew the ups and downs in Anne's life. But ... she didn't let it be known, her ups and downs, because she had joy and that's a joy that nobody can give you but the Lord. See only God can give you that joy. Your job, nothing else can give you the joy that Anne Pressly, Ron Hoof or Paul Eells had. That is a special joy and if we take from Anne the good and that happiness that would make us all better people. Anne was young enough to be my daughter, but I learned so much from her. You know a lot of people say it ain't how long you live, but it's what you do in your lifetime. Anne as a young person did more in her life than a lot of people would do in 80, 90 years."

—*Marcus McDonald, KATV photojournalist*

"Good times, sweet friend. I miss you, but I know we'll see each other again. Love ya, mean it!!"

—*Sandra Kirk, KLRT reporter*

"I can't look at a magazine in the check-out line without thinking about Anne. I can't look at the color pink without thinking about Anne. I can't pick up a cell phone without thinking about Anne (we loved our gadgets.) I can't watch a cardboard boat race without thinking about Anne. I can't look at a hovercraft without thinking about Anne. Everyday I look across the newsroom and I see her empty desk and a lump builds in my throat. How could this happen? I just hope she knew that I rode her so hard not because I didn't care, but because I knew her stories mattered and that people connected with her and I truly felt she connected with others. Anne, I'm honored I got the chance to play a small part in your life, because you will always fill a big place in mine. Love you ... and I truly mean it."

—*Patrick Green, KATV producer*

"From the moment I walked in she made me feel so special and welcome, which is a theme at our station, but I think it was really spearheaded by her. She had that way of making the stranger on the street feel special, anybody she was interviewing, and even her closest friends. And that's one of the things about her I hope lives on in the rest of us."

—*Shilo Groover Korzen, KATV producer*

Shilo Groover Korzen, Jessica Dean, Anne and Heather Crawford

> "**A**nne as a young person did more in her life than a lot of people would do in 80, 90 years."
> —*Marcus McDonald*

"When someone so fun and so attractive and with such an attractive spirit is taken, I always try to figure out why. Why Anne? why Paul? Whoever. Anne was a very attractive person and spirit-wise you were drawn to her. She didn't share her faith openly unless you asked her. If you asked her, she was ready and prepared to talk about her faith, but she wasn't the initiator of that conversation. I think that because she was so well-liked and her funeral was so well-attended and the gospel at her funeral was so clearly presented, I think that is one way that helps explain why she left us at such a young age. I think that there were people saved at her service. I know there were people blessed by her young and healthy organs. I've been able to find a few things that might explain why and [they] have been comforting to me. She's missed, but she did a lot of good while she was here."

—*Jason Pederson, KATV consumer reporter*

"I loved working with her and I miss her dearly. There's not a day that goes by when I'm riding around town whenever we're going to a news story ... there's always something that reminds me of her. I think about her all the time. It still seems unreal that she's not here with us, but she's here with us in spirit. Because you remember all the laughter."

—*Ray Hamilton, KATV photojournalist*

"One my favorites is how Anne's weave ended up in my hair! Being the fashion maven she was, I considered her one of my go-to gals for anything dealing with hair, make-up and clothes. Which leads me to a memory I will always hold dear. Anne died just two months before my wedding day, but a piece of her was there. Literally. Months before, I e-mailed her and asked if she knew a stylist that could do my hair for the wedding. She recommended hers. Anne had just had her hair done for another wedding and ordered a pack of extensions and split them with her stylist, Sarah. When I went in, Sarah pulled a few of them out and said, "I thought we would put these in, so a little piece of Anne will be there too." I almost burst into tears right there in the salon. At the wedding, I remember, I told friends that Anne's extensions are here, in my hair, can you believe it??!! Jessica Dean kissed my hair and said, "She is here." We all laughed and cried about it that night. I know she would've loved that."

—*Sandra Kirk, KLRT reporter*

"Forever will my heart smile when I think of my times with 'White Barbie'!"
—*Tomeca Sloan, former KATV producer*

"I had encouraged Anne and given her advice over the years (professionally and personally)as I watched her grow and mature. But I never would have guessed that in the end...she would be the one teaching me. To be honest, working with Anne sometimes took some patience. Her zest for life would sometimes bubble over and get in the way of quiet concentration at work. And yet now, I'd give anything to have her loud and entertaining outbursts back. Anne taught me to have fun. And more importantly, to find fun. To not hold back and to embrace others when they're having fun. In the end, the fun moments are what we all remember the most. She took her job seriously and did it very well, but she didn't take herself too seriously. She really lived every day to the fullest...and has taught me to do the same. We miss you Anne. Thanks for teaching us to grab life by the reigns and hold on for the ride. You sure did. Your life lives on in all of us."

—*Christina Muñoz, KATV news anchor*

Early in the morning of July 13, 2009, a small group of Anne's friends gathered in front of the small frame house where she had lived. They were there for remembrance and closure. After months on the market, the abandoned residence had sold and the buyers chose to clear the lot. A light mist fell as the bulldozer razed the structure. Anne's friends quietly watched holding pink balloons. They huddled together for a brief prayer and a moment of silence. The pink cluster was released skyward. A single balloon lingered behind the others, and then drifted up slowly. Almost as if Anne was bidding a final farewell.